ENCOUNTERS AT THE COUNTER

What Congregations Can Learn about Hospitality from Business

ALAN JOHNSON

THE PILGRIM PRESS
CLEVELAND

The Pilgrim Press, 700 Prospect Avenue, Cleveland, Ohio 44115
thepilgrimpress.com
© 2009 Alan Johnson

Scripture quotations, unless otherwise noted, are from the New Revised Standard Version of the Bible, © 1989 by the Division of Christian Education of the National Council of Churches of Christ in the United States of America and are used by permission. Changes have been made for inclusivity.

All rights reserved. Published 2009

Printed in the United States of America on acid-free paper

13   12   11   10   09   5   4   3   2

Library of Congress Cataloging-in-Publication Data

Johnson, Alan, 1943–
    Encounters at the counter : what congregations can learn about hospitality from business / Alan Johnson.
        p. cm.
    ISBN 978-0-8298-1817-8 (alk. paper)
    1. Church greeters.   2. Hospitality—Religious aspects—Christianity.
3. Customer services.   I. Title.
BV705.J59 2009
259—dc22   2009002978

ENCOUNTERS
AT THE
COUNTER

CONTENTS

FOREWORD

Alan Johnson has written a winsome reflection on the practice of hospitality and has done so with cunning, precise narrative specificity. His book puts me in mind of *Duffy's Tavern*, an ancient radio show from my young years. Each episode of the series began with a phone ringing. The answering voice always said, "Duffy's Tavern, where the elite meet to eat; Duffy ain't here . . . Oh, hello, Duffy." It was always the owner who called. And then each narrative episode unfolded with a drama about the folk who moved in and out of the tavern. Of course they were not "elite." They were quite ordinary people, likely working-class folk whose interests turned on their daily lives. But in Duffy's Tavern, they were for the moment the elite. They were taken seriously by the script writers, and every morsel of food taken was offered as a banquet fit for a king.

Alan Johnson knows about that sort of contact that makes one elite (for a moment); he brings to his report a grace and a dignity that reflects engagement with and respect for his "customers." He reflects on a year of experience in a bread store, where he served as a welcomer. He paid attention to the folk who came in for bread and other food, and he took and takes them seriously. The contacts he was able to have were fleeting, but nonetheless important, because, as Alan understands in profound ways, everyone wants and needs to have attention paid. Alan's heart and work is always in the church, and so he reflects on what is portable from his business experience to and for the life of the church. He makes it quite clear that the church has much to learn that is already known and practiced in business, in moving beyond "greeters" and "ushers" to authentic welcomers.

The narrative specificity of this book spins off to big questions in many directions. Here I mention two such big issues. First, that our dog-eat-dog rat-race society is perfectly organized against welcoming hospitality. We are so into merit and performance and quid-pro-quo and no free lunch that there is among us very little time or energy for welcome that is not manipulative and exploitative. The issue is systemic and provides acute reasons why people need to be recognized and are glad for fleeting welcome. Alan's action as a welcomer and the more general action of welcome that he proposes are deeply subversive of the way our particular world of anxiety functions.

Second, there is no doubt that the hunger for hospitality is a pervasive creaturely need. We know it ourselves and we see it in our pets, as with our cats, who purr when attention is paid. Given that "cosmic reality," it is nonetheless the case that the matter of welcoming hospitality is the peculiar domain of the church. Indeed Jesus upbraids his disciples for forgetting the bread (Mark 8:15–16). They forgot the bread because they did not understand that being with Jesus put them in the bread business, in the business of feeding and welcoming and noticing human hunger. Not unlike Alan, the disciples are at work in the Bread Company.

The church's commitment to the bread business is peculiarly enacted in the Eucharist, the giving of broken bread. In that awesome moment of exchange when bread is given and received with holy words, it is bread and body and truth and hope and compassion and forgiveness and welcome that are passed around for all to share. Alan of course knows that it is not about the bread; but of course he also knows that it is precisely about the bread. It is and it is not. It is that "is/is not" reality that makes the welcoming moment so laden with thick potential, because when we share, we share more than we have at hand. It is the sharing of memories and hopes and cadences that are central to our common life. In fact, the actual exchange at the Eucharist is a fleeting moment and then it is time to move to the next thing. The actual instant of "communion" in the Eucharist is as brief and as fleeting as the exchanges that Alan had at the counter. Perhaps all such laden instances are only for a moment, and then it is time to move on, to move on in the church to mission, to move on in the bread company to the duties of the day, to move on refreshed and, in ways that we cannot explain, transformed.

This narrative report on welcome is situated *exactly in our anti-welcome society* and is addressed *exactly to the church* in its vocation as a welcomer. Readers will want to reflect on how and why the church has such a hard time performing this most elemental act that is entrusted to it. The reason that welcoming does not come easily, surely, is that the church, like the world, is occupied by anxious folk who fear "the other," who is unlike us. Thus conservatives do not easily welcome progressives and progressives do not easily welcome conservatives. For reasons of anxiety, perhaps, the church has been distorted by custom and habit, distracted by doctrine and piety and polity and liturgy and ideologies of all sorts that draw us away from this most simple, direct, and elemental act of welcome.

This book is a summons about going back to basics. The book has a powerful pull on us, partly because of the tales Alan has to tell. Beyond that, all those who know Alan will attest that he himself is a quintessential welcoming agent for God's reign. Thus the author's own inclination is as revelatory as is the narrative report about this elemental human act. We can see in the book Alan's own readiness to knead the bread and to notice that the food supply of our particular tribe has no trademark, no identifying brand. That bread, filtered through our tribe, is not tribal bread, and, therefore, it is a gift. Before the gift we are recipients, and then we are givers. Bread creates safe meeting places. We have been warned by Jesus about the ersatz bread and the phony welcome of the Herodians and the Pharisees. This offer is real nourishment. Duffy would be glad for this book, because he would know that when we eat gift-bread, we are all made elite . . . and satisfied!

Walter Brueggemann
Columbia Theological Seminary

P R E F A C E

The way I began to work at the Great Harvest Bread Company in customer service was by chance or by what I call a God-incident. An ordained minister, I had been a chaplain at the Children's Hospital in Denver till I decided to join my wife on her three-month sabbatical in Italy, Greece, and northern California, which meant resigning as chaplain at the hospital. My work there had been deeply meaningful, touching, and engaging to me. Although disappointing to me in some ways, my decision to resign would, I knew, also open a door to new possibilities.

During those months after we returned from the sabbatical, I filled out job applications and had interviews but still did not find the right job. My thirty-eight years of ordained ministry, including sixteen years developing and implementing a national program for our denomination and seven years of hospital chaplaincy, did not seem to lead to any appropriate opportunity. The doors continued to close at hospitals, hospices, and at a children's home.

One day while leafing through the want ads in our local paper, I noticed that a local bread company wanted a part-time customer service staff person. Since one of the foci of my ministry had been training, teaching, and writing about hospitality for congregations, I was drawn to customer service. I love being around food, people, and baking. Over the years, I have taken cooking classes at Zona Spray's Cooking School in Hudson, Ohio, and have also been a volunteer front assistant at the local Culinary Institute of the Rockies, Boulder, Colorado, for more than three years. During our sabbatical, I took cooking classes from Donatella in Cortona, Italy. One of my "research projects" was to taste biscotti across Italy in order to compare them with my own. This has led to selling my "Beloved Biscotti" to local coffee shops. But that is another story.

So I went to the job interview at the Great Harvest Bread Company in Boulder and got the job. It gave me several days a week when I would have a schedule. It freed me up to write, to train for several races, and to spend more time in my congregation's activities. I began to understand that the job could be fulfilling rather than just filling up time. As the months unfolded, I worked one, two, or three days a week, six hours a day.

This book began on the evening of my wife's first art show as we were driving from Boulder to Denver after my first day working at the bread company. I was sharing some of the stories I had heard that day. Customers tended to share brief comments, and I found myself asking a couple of questions and responding to their stories by sharing my own experiences. It was fun and energizing. My wife suggested I write those conversations down, and that is how this book began. Every day for the more than one year I was working at Great Harvest, I kept notes in a small notebook, entered my reflections manually into a journal, and then typed them into my computer.

Seeing the confluence of my work experiences of hospitality with my congregational experiences of hospitality was a delightful surprise. What are the lessons for a congregation's hospitality as a result of my being in customer service in a business? And what could small businesses learn about customer service from observing a congregation's spirituality in action in their practices of hospitality?

I have had other influences, too. In particular, I deeply appreciate my encounters with the late Henri Nouwen, who taught me by example and through his writings about the profound gift of hospitality. With the eyes of the heart, I learned from Henri to see the world in new ways, especially as regards those who are marginalized or are strangers. Likewise, the books by John A. Sanford have grounded my understanding of spirituality. My spirit is nurtured by the way he amplifies stories from the Hebrew Scripture through Jungian insights.

I am enormously grateful to my wife, Martie McMane, who has spurred me on as I explored new work situations. My abiding love goes to her. She gave me the freedom and encouragement that allowed me to work at the counter and to work on this book. She also has a lovingly critical eye as the person who first read what I wrote with candor and affection. For that, I thank her.

I am grateful to the late Robert L. Burt for his tenacious leadership with the United Church Board for Homeland Ministry. Bob gave me support and encouragement to explore, write, and teach about the ministry of hospitality throughout the United Church of Christ in the 1980s and early '90s.

I extend my thanks to Kim Martin Sadler of The Pilgrim Press, who first encouraged me to write the book and submit a manuscript. It was an opening door for which I am grateful. When I learned that the editor who would work on the manuscript for this book was the same person who was the editor of the book I had worked on with Mortimer Arias, entitled *The Great Commission,* I was thrilled. Ulrike Guthrie was a Godsend who was able to trim, clarify, and structure my writing with personal incisiveness. Whatever sings in this book, she has helped be heard.

I thank the congregations of which I have been a part where hospitality became a reality in the on-goingness of ministry. It's one thing to talk a good line, but the translation into action takes determination and persistence along with imagination. Coming from teaching the ministry of hospitality throughout the United Church of Christ to living that hospitality in the trenches of a local congregation, I thank the Saugatuck Congregational Church, Westport, Connecticut. For my ten years of being part of the formation of the Membership Committee and embodying the ministry of hospitality at the First Congregational Church, United Church of Christ, Boulder, Colorado, as a member, I am greatly appreciative. I extend particular thanks to those who have served on that committee and everyone in that congregation who embraced welcoming strangers and one another as a mark of Christian hospitality.

The guidance of God, I believe, has been at work in my work. Going from employment to unemployment and then to working again has sometimes been arduous. Yet looking back at the path that I had not planned but that I have come to trust, I can see that when my energy converges with new opportunities in front of me, I grow, and for that I am grateful.

INTRODUCTION

A s I worked at the Great Harvest Bread Company, it became clear to me that customer service was paramount and that the key to good customer service is hospitality. For sixteen years, I had traveled the United States teaching hospitality to United Church of Christ congregations, so I was familiar with some of its practices. Coming to this work in the business world as an ordained minister, I brought a spiritual perspective to hospitality in customer service. But my primary goal is to help congregations extend their hospitality. The encounters at the bread counter are very brief. Yet making human connections there is possible, as it is also in congregations.

Hospitality in a congregation is about welcoming the other into a safe place; customer service is about greeting the other in a pleasant environment. The goal of the congregation is to draw the visitor or member into an authentic relationship with the Holy. The goal of the business is to know the customer and to offer the services that might meet the customer's acknowledged or as yet unacknowledged needs.

This book is not a "how to" book for congregations about hospitality, although it contains plenty of practical suggestions for you to make your congregation more welcoming, as does the accompanying online study guide (available at ucccresources.com). My encounters at the counter do, however, suggest many ways we can adopt and adapt insights from the business world to the world of the congregation. Yet none of this is particularly difficult. St. Paul talks about it simply as "extend[ing] hospitality to strangers."[1] Welcoming is action. Arthur Sutherland writes, "By adopting the vision of Jesus, by seeing as and how Jesus sees, our inclination toward hospitality will become natural and unforced."[2] I rather think that the way to practice and extend hospitality comes through just doing it.

Many congregations find it difficult to be hospitable. It is not that they do not know what to do; it is just that they don't do it. Even though they have heard the biblical stories about Jesus and have been encouraged in the name of Christ to offer the welcome that they themselves have received, many of us still find it unnatural or awkward to welcome the stranger. This book immerses congregations in very visible ways to offer the kind of hospitality I have experienced at the bread company. Hospitality is one way to put love into action.

PART ONE | PRACTICING ENCOUNTER

I

SHOWING YOUR SPIRITUALITY IN YOUR HOSPITALITY

Spirituality relates to that dimension of our-
selves as human beings which erects frameworks
of meaning that provide a motivating force to
our lives. Spirituality is associated with the
pilgrimage of life; connection with other people
and the natural world; a sense of the sacred; and
a reaching out to something beyond ourselves.

—PETER DUNCAN GILBERT[1]

FOR ME SPIRITUALITY IS IN RELATIONSHIPS, AND RELATIONSHIPS COME
through connections. Since we are born from relationship and into
relationship, perhaps the best way to know who we are is through
being in relationship. We are who we are because we are in relationship with our true self, with our family, friends, spouse, or partner.
We are who we are in relationship with our work, our vocation, and
our calling. We are who we are in relationship with the sacred and
whatever and whoever is beyond ourselves. We meet the Holy in all
these relationships, for our spirituality shows in connection.

3

What is spirituality but a connection with a power deep within us that is echoed in the world outside of us? It is of course also the reverse: a connection with a power greater than we are that is outside of our self but that is also echoed deeply within us. The Holy becomes real in those encounters.

Henri Nouwen writes that "the spiritual life [means] the nurturing of the eternal amid the temporal, the lasting within the passing, God's presence in the human family. It is the life of the divine Spirit within us."[2] Seeking this mysterious presence is a spiritual quest. We cannot prove everyone has a religion gene. However, we can know there is something beyond our selves. Perhaps it is through love, or the intricacies of the body, or the wonder of nature, or the capacity and the will to survive. Such qualities can be experienced and appreciated even if they are not always understood.

So when we encounter this real connection with an other, we experience a fleeting connection with the Spirit. The bread counter at the store is like a table at which food is available and at which people gather to be fed, by stories and relationships as well as actual food. Food is available; people gather in front of it; and stories are told. "Every meal, like every encounter with a human being, has the potential to reveal God present in Creation. The table represents the unknown yearning of every human heart for communion with 'something more' that infuses all that exists."[3] That "something more" is that ingredient of spirituality that is made real in the encounter with the person and the bread.

Father Divine used the word "tangibilitate" on one of his radio shows in Chicago many years ago to describe making a thought, an idea, or even a vision real and tangible. At the bread company, I learned to offer human contact along with an excellent product. Spirituality combines the earthly with the heavenly; it blends the tactile stuff of bread with the connection of what is holy; it brings more life out of what just is. That is to tangibilitate. The spiritual encounter may come through a warm and a gracious welcome, but it is more than the nod and the smile and the greeting. The connection is made when the interaction between two people feels larger than just the two of them being in proximity to each other.

One afternoon it was slow at the counter. Ann, a middle-aged woman, came to the door and I greeted her with open arms as I stood behind the counter. When she saw my arms wide and lifted up, she stopped in her tracks and smiled, raising her arms, too. She felt cared for and connected.

Welcoming the day, welcoming the one before us, being in the present moment, and opening ourselves to the experience of what is—are all spiritual disciplines.

SPIRITUAL DISCIPLINES FOR HOSPITALITY

Henri Nouwen describes disciplines as ways of leaving "room in our hearts where we can listen to the Spirit of God in a life changing way. We guard space in our lives to become sensitive and receptive to God's word."[4]

The practice of making room for the encounter to happen is essential in the hospitality of a business and a congregation, but it can happen in many different ways. Some make room through prayer and meditation. Many people think of those practices first when they think of spirituality. Others make room for that encounter, that spirituality, in nature. Here in Boulder, where I live, being outside is the name of the game. Some people here consider walking on a hillside, hiking in the mountains, fly fishing, running, cycling, swimming in lakes, kayaking in rivers, rock climbing, and skiing as spiritual disciplines. Other people would include worship, reading, journaling, yoga, having a great meal with friends or family, singing in a choir, making art, serving a meal to the hungry, listening to music, going to a concert, seeing a movie, or going on a retreat. Any of these activities can become a spiritual discipline if it is done attentively. Attentiveness and intention give some space around the activity. It is like having an "observer" in your own mind that looks at what you are doing. In that observation, you can appreciate what you are doing and what is going on around you as well as what is going on inside you.

One person's spiritual disciplines or ways of being attentive are different from the next. But in each case, such attentiveness means allowing the space that is needed for an encounter. Without that space, genuine encounter and genuine hospitality are hard pressed to happen.

Congregations are well placed to foster the exercising of members' spiritual disciplines so hospitality can be extended, not least because spirituality is both an individual and a communal practice. For example, because congregations are confessional contexts—places where we confess or declare what we believe—we get practice in community saying things that are real, honest, and sometimes difficult. Confession means being authentic with each other. Such authenticity is promoted in a situation of trust, and then speaking the truth becomes energizing. Most of us know when someone is being phony, when what that person is saying is not true. Trust is built over time, and when it is there, one can speak the truth. Regular customers at the bread company have learned that they can trust the staff and the product. First-time customers need a staff person to extend trust and welcome to them. The same goes for visitors to our churches.

Sometimes that extension of trust and welcome actually means giving someone space to be. One day I noticed that a colleague at the counter appeared downcast. I asked what was going on. "I am down on myself today," he said. That staff member was self-absorbed to the point of being withdrawn. He was not himself. We gave him some space, letting him acknowledge his feeling. He did recover and came back to engage with customers at the counter. The love towards self translates to love for others. The staff person had to pay attention to his own mental and emotional state before he could find a way back out and then connect authentically again with his customers. This can be a deep and costly exploration, of course, but it is essential if we are to live authentic lives.

What about my customers: Will I ever see them again? We greet one another at the counter, then say goodbye and often our paths never cross a second time. Others are regular customers and we can connect more immediately, especially if each of us can remember something that we had shared before. Still, even those encounters end or are interrupted. So we learn to enjoy the exchange, share a story, carry a burden or welcome a blessing, and let that be sufficient.

The spiritual discipline of walking a labyrinth is an example of how I experienced my time behind the counter. A labyrinth is not a maze. It is a circling pattern on the ground on which one walks from the entrance through a circuitous path to the center. You will not get lost as long as you stay on the path. It is a spiritual practice. One of my experiences in walking the labyrinth is that although some people may have begun before me, there are times when it seems that we are walking side by side on different paths. Then all of a sudden they or I turn and we are not walking together. That person and I may never meet again in this labyrinth. We have silently spoken a hello and a goodbye without words.

Meeting people at the counter and then seeing them leave the counter is a constant reminder of the fleeting time we have together. Not wanting to make a connection is a loss of an affirmation of our common humanness. Not wanting them to go is a loss of an affirmation of our unique individuality. Coming and going is the rhythm of living. Nouwen writes, "In our relationships with one another, sometimes we act as though we prefer the illusion that we live immortally. We forget that we will see each other only for a relatively short time. That you or I might not be here tomorrow, next week, or next year. And so we avoid death rather than value life for all its preciousness."[5]

As I leave the labyrinth, having paid attention to my walking and having been at the center, I am more aware of how I will reenter society. As I leave work, I am energized by the connections that have come to me as I have worked those hours and acknowledged the center that is present, not only for me, but for each of us. The preciousness of greeting people on my walk and in my work reminds me to pay attention to what is right in front of me when those people leave to be on their own walk. In our own mortality, the gift of the present, albeit fleeting, points to the home that beckons those who are on the path of Christian faith.

For most Christians who are reading this book, that spiritual home is most concretely in their faith community. The words and rituals of the congregation's services convey the quality of spirituality that makes a space, a place that is sacred or holy. While much of the learning about spirituality in a congregation will be through its corporate activities, such as worship, fellowship, education and outreach/mission, it also includes those spiritual practices of prayer, singing, retreats, devotional reading, walking the labyrinth, listening, and journaling. Through these disciplines one nourishes the core of one's faith. It is where one forms the eyes of faith to see the world in a particular way. It is important for the specific practices to be incorporated into the services of the congregation on a regular basis. For example, the pastoral prayer in a worship service could include prayers for those who are visiting and could include those who feel excluded. In addition, there could be specific spiritual practices focused on those who are set aside for the ministry of hospitality, such as learning how to be a good listener, an active listener. This could be offered for those who are asked to create that inner space so that the other person may be invited into a welcoming and gracious place.

While our spiritual practices are intended to provide succor and encouragement, sometimes they are not immediately comforting. These practices may pull us in directions that we had not intended to go. It is not always an immediate comfort to experience spirituality. "Genuine spirituality is not cozy, and seldom makes you comfortable. It challenges, disturbs, unsettles, and leaves you feeling like someone is at the center of your existence on a major remodeling mission. While affirming how wonderful you are, better than you really know, spirituality is also meant to change you. If it doesn't it is something less than spirituality."[6]

For example, when our congregation decided to relocate two families and four teenagers from Kosovo in the late 1990s, it was empowering to realize we could welcome them to a place where they would escape the immediate dangers of war, but it also became profoundly unsettling. On the television we had seen the miles and miles of people walking on the roads leaving their homes with only a few possessions on their backs. We could not begin to fathom the suffering and pain they were experiencing. Our hearts were opened by that vision. In a very small way we took their pain into our hearts.

This capacity for hospitality was then radically expanded as my wife and I hosted a family of father and mother and three children under five years old, who lived with us for eight months. We did not speak each other's language. We were Christian clergy and they were Muslims. They all wanted to sleep in one large room, and for many months we were barely able to offer solace to their fears and comfort for the nightmares they had from their departure from their homes in Kosovo. Yet, in those months, we practiced hospitality in ways that gave us deep spiritual connections with this family, and we received the bounty of blessings.

Beyond these efforts of our own, it was the congregation's hospitality that was transforming. This hospitality included offering language classes, medical appointments, transportation, jobs, picnics, and gatherings with other Kosovo refugees who were in the area. Whether those experiences were simple or difficult, all of us were transformed by them.

In the congregation, paying attention to the foundations of one's spirituality—and therefore the foundations of one's faith—leads to a more genuine, authentic, and embracing hospitality. The basis of our Christian faith is that God has first loved us (1 John 4:19). Knowing that one is loved from the beginning, knowing that one has been loved first, makes it possible for one to love others. Besides, it is an imperative, a command: "Beloved, since God loved us so much, we also ought to love one another" (1 John 4:11) This is the context in which a relationship is formed. The connection is made. Divine love shapes our lives and the relationships we have with others. This is true in our congregations; it is true at the counter! From the web of connection that is made through the disciplines of spirituality, the blessings flow as hospitality is extended.

BARRIERS TO HOSPITALITY

Yet we all know as well that certain things impede hospitality in a business and at church. As people enter the store, from behind the counter staff exude an attitude of attentiveness and love, while also being aware of the customer's needs. Here, the physical counter itself can be both a helpful barrier and an obstacle. On the one hand, the counter can be a boundary so that my enthusiasms will not bowl over the customer. Whether the customer is new or familiar, some will want to maintain their distance while others will welcome a physical or verbal approach. So on the other hand, when I come out from behind the counter, if I have "read" the customer right, I remove the barrier and allow an immediacy and a presence facilitated by physical proximity. Without the counter between us, we choose how close to stand. Usually I come out from behind the counter to point to the different breads and to ask my customer what he or she is looking for. But my physical moving toward the customer can also offer the customer an occasion and the safety to share a little more about herself or himself.

A woman overwhelmed by the myriad bread choices was talking with me about what constitutes helpful limits. "Limits and boundaries are good," I said. "It's like the experiment in which a playground was deliberately built without a fence; the thinking was that a fence would restrict the children. When the children did not know where the boundaries were, they would typically huddle in the middle and not play. It actually restricted their freedom. The boundaries represented the perimeter of security and the outer limits of freedom. When the boundaries came down, the students' freedoms were lost.[7] The boundary brought freedom," I said. As this woman was facing the choices of breads, our conversation was able to focus on what type of bread she was interested in, and what ingredients might be most suitable for her. This concept of having boundaries, limits, or a more focused discussion seemed to help her make choices about the breads in front of her. Acknowledging the visible and the invisible boundaries, the limits and the options, can allow the encounter to be more appropriate.

There are also boundaries in the roles that people have in the congregation. While there may not be a physical barrier there such as a counter, the variety of roles may clarify the way people interact. At the bread company, there are customers and staff. In the congregation, there can be a distinction between a greeter, an usher, and a welcomer, depending on the size of the congregation. These roles indi-

cate particular responsibilities and they delineate the type of relationship that is formed. Clarifying these responsibilities may make
the interaction understandable if not also comfortable. In the congregation, the larger the attendance, the more important it is to dif-
ferentiate those roles. Visitors can be unnerved by not knowing
where to go, where to sit, and, if they bring children, what is appropriate for their children. Having at least the following roles fulfilled
in the church demonstrates hospitality in action:

1. The *greeter* welcomes everyone, usually with a smile and a
   handshake.

2. It usually is the *usher* who hands out a bulletin or program.
   The bulletin might be a barrier or it might be a way to connect. Part of that depends on the intention and the attitude of
   the person offering it. The bulletin may be given without
   even looking at the person receiving it, or the usher may give
   the program without first offering a handshake. The lack of
   such a gesture itself creates a distance between people. On
   the other hand, if the usher offers a warm greeting and a
   handshake and then gives the bulletin, a beginning connection is already made. The usher may also have surveyed
   where there are spaces for the visitor to sit, may ask the visitor's preference, or may notice that the visitor has already selected where she or he would like sit.

3. The *welcomer* is the one who will be attentive to how to
   help visitors experience a warm and appropriate welcome,
   being available to orient visitors, give them any information
   they might find helpful—such as the congregation's mission
   statement, newsletter, list of activities and small group experiences, or staff business cards—and if possible get information
   from them to make a hospitable follow-up conversation by
   phone, email, or visit.

These roles and responsibilities do help establish the parameters
of at least the beginning of the relationship between the member and

the visitor or newcomer. As in the example of the children's playground without a fence, when we act as if there are no boundaries in our interactions with others, the relationship will not be optimally productive or healthy. "Boundaries allow us to give more to others, not less. Boundaries do not exclude the other; in fact, if you become a person with actual boundaries, you are better able to give to other people because you do not feel diminished by it. . . . Boundaries keep us from feeling used or manipulated."[8] Hospitality needs to have the tensile strength of a spirituality that knows about boundaries without creating barriers that prevent hospitality.

Barriers or boundaries are not intended to block relationships from developing, but to enhance them. When the staff person is comfortable in his or her own skin, the boundary can offer the container in which the fullness and the appropriateness of the relationship can develop. This is true in the congregation, too. When one's spiritual life is enhanced and embraced, then offering hospitality means being true to oneself. Meeting the other person where that person is can only happen when one is clear about where one is in the encounter. "Opening up to others does not mean you let some one trample all over you. It does not mean you let people rip chunks off of you. It does not mean you cease to take care of yourself or do what you need to do to remain emotionally, physically, and spiritually healthy. We can give simple kindness without losing ourselves."[9] Boundaries provide the container for the spiritual energy to flow. This is why practicing a variety of spiritual disciplines will build up the internal strength of the people who are welcoming others. There needs to be someone there, someone who is really present when extending a welcome, and each person doing the welcoming has a particular role and responsibility for creating genuine hospitality. What might those roles and responsibilities be?

DISCERNING SKILLS AND RECRUITING FOR HOSPITALITY

It is obviously best to enlist as welcomers people who actually enjoy other people! Ask yourself: is the person you're considering for the job one who engages warmly in conversation? Does she make eye contact when speaking and listening? Does he listen? Practicing these skills in your congregation is a great idea—for example, in role play paying attention to tone of voice, eye contact, the physical distance between people, body posture, using one's arms, and the smile.

What if you need to recruit more welcomers? Advertising is one way that a business seeks to find employees. One of the ads for customer service staff at the bread company goes this way. "We need more nice people w/ excellent customer service skills. Must be self motivated & happy." How do you train happy people? I wondered. One author who has focused on the blend of finding persons with skills and training them is Danny Meyer. Meyer has opened several restaurants in New York City, and his book *Setting the Table: The Transforming Power of Hospitality in Business* offers insights about hospitality in that industry that are also applicable to congregations.

Meyer writes, "the trick to delivering superior hospitality was to hire genuine, happy, optimistic people."[10] This is not easy to do. He writes that what he wants is "the kind of people on my team who naturally radiate warmth, friendliness, happiness and kindness. It feels genuinely good to be around them. There's an upbeat feeling, a twinkle in the eye, a dazzling sparkle from within."[11] He lists five core emotional skills that he looks for as he hires: "Optimistic warmth (a sense that the glass is always at *least* half full), intelligence (not just 'smarts' but an insatiable curiosity to learn for the sake of learning), work ethic, empathy, and self-awareness and integrity (an understanding of what makes you tick)"[12] Although these qualities are typically either there or not, discovering them can take time.

It is important for the person hiring the customer service staff as well as those who are inviting the welcomers in a congregation to realize that those qualities that cannot be trained for are still significant. It reminds me of the phrase in a Ford Foundation study on leadership that is very similar to finding a left-handed fastballer. Just as you cannot train a left-handed pitcher to have a fastball, you cannot train a leader. You just have to have the qualities of being a left-handed fastball pitcher and the same goes for a leader. One person put it, "Leadership is the ability to influence, to focus the acts and thoughts of others . . . there must be characteristics that appeal to his (or her) immediate peers. I think the characteristics are the same at every level—charisma, confidence, courage, some tolerance for ambiguity, things like that. Now, I'm not sure how much you can train those qualities, but you can support them with information and experience."[13]

Just as you cannot train a left-handed pitcher to throw a fastball, perhaps that is true with happy customer staff and the competent welcomers in the congregation. You cannot train the happy factor. The way Kris Thompson put it is, "You can teach people any technical skill, but you can't teach them how to be a kindhearted, generous-minded person with an open spirit."[14] Hire the right ones, involve capable people in the congregation's ministry of hospitality, and it works.

Does this mean that any member of a congregation who wants to be involved in a hospitality ministry, or who just wants to *be* hospitable has to have what Meyer calls "dazzling sparkle," or be "radiating warmth," or have a great pitching arm? Some of us are not naturally drawn to engage other people, to acknowledge them, or to create that space for the connection to occur. There are some people who can be very quietly welcoming to others if they are the ones approached; they are just not going to do the approaching. However, their very being can be a welcoming place for the stranger and the friend. Might they have spiritual strength to offer others? Yes! It is just that they are not usually going to be the front-line welcomers.

Finding the people to embody and exude the "front-line" type of hospitality in our congregations takes discernment. But just as a baseball team is not made up of all left-handed fastball pitchers, the congregation is not made up of all front-line welcomers. As the scripture indicates, it takes different parts to make a whole body. Not everyone has the gift of hospitality. Discerning, nurturing, and then freeing the gift of hospitality in the congregation becomes the role of the people who have the eyes to see, the heart to know, and the wisdom to call it forth. However, in many congregations there is a low priority on hospitality or the members feel they are already sufficiently friendly and welcoming when in fact they are not. Meyer's guidelines about the five needed skills of optimistic warmth, intelligence (insatiable curiosity), work ethic, empathy, and self-awareness and integrity are therefore also helpful as we consider the ministry of hospitality in our congregations.

FINDING MEANING IN HOSPITALITY

Spiritual practices by customer service staff as well as members of a congregation can lead to a meaningful encounter. I need meaning to make sense of who I am and what I do. If I were at the bread company just to have something to do or to fill up a void in my life, I would probably shrivel up in spirit. Rather, I want to experience meaning in what I do, even in each encounter at the counter. After having been a chaplain at a children's hospital, where I encountered and counseled many families of children with life-limiting illnesses, I found it quite a contrast being at a cheerful place behind a counter serving bread. Yet both have meaning. Those who come into the bread store are carrying their own troubles, burdens, and needs. Especially as the downturn in the world's economy brings a high level of stress, our interactions with one another may offer some respite, some comfort, and some empathetic support. William Sloane Coffin warns us "never to have an experience and miss the meaning."[15] It takes focus to look for meaning in customer service since there is one exchange after another. Looking for the meaning can be exhausting or exhilarating. Even a simple "welcome" as a customer enters or a "thank you" and "I hope to see you here again" as the customer leaves is a way of recognizing the other person's humanity. Such welcoming and gracious expressions weave a fabric of meaning and connections with others.

In my work as an ordained minister, I have appreciated deep human connections and shared meaning, perhaps particularly when in those human relationships we encountered conflict and uncomfortable situations. Perhaps our shared meanings are more obvious and visible in ministry settings of church, hospital, and home than at a business that has neither IV poles nor religious symbols as part of the décor. Yet, if the occasion presents itself and if the context is conducive, conversation can lead to discovering the meaning that is present anywhere and anytime.

While there may be similarities in many settings, however, there are dissimilarities as well. In retail, I could set aside the job. I did not bring anything home except stories and a loaf of bread. As a chaplain, even when I was not at the hospital, I continued to think about children I had met there and their families. The encounters at the bread company were usually much briefer, not as deep, and did not continue over time and so allow me to get to know people better.

Comparing my work as chaplain with being in customer service, however, has revealed some similarities. Both are about caring for each person as an individual. Both involve as much as possible bringing my authentic self to each encounter. In both I offer something of value, either a presence or a product, both of which are valuable. The good news I have in me is the deep well of hope that affirms meaning in life in both the store and in the hospital. I believe that is possible for everyone. I might not have had as much opportunity to share that hope and meaning verbally at the bread counter; however, I could affirm it in my own way of being present with customers, as I had with patients and their families in the hospital. For wherever there is a real connection with another person—in the store, in the hospital, or in our congregations—there is good news. When humans connect, hope and meaning are made manifest.

One afternoon in the store, Evelyn, a customer, came in looking for a bread sample. We began to talk and I shared that I was reflecting on my experience of working at Great Harvest Bread Company and was thinking about writing this book. I told her that I had as a working title *Better Than Sliced Bread: Life's Lessons in the Bread Company.* "What about a different title," she volunteered, "such as, *It's Not about the Bread.*" I liked that because although it is important that the product is good and worthwhile and even needed, another ingredient for me had become the relationship and connection with people that I was experiencing at the counter. It may be that along with the actual desire and need for the bread in their day they also needed to be perked up, encouraged, or acknowledged. The exchange could be humane and even humorous, not just a transaction of goods. The engagement at the counter for me included forming friendships, making a difference in someone's life, starting connections with meaning or humor, acknowledging the worth and validity of each person, discovering some truth from a customer, affirming the uniqueness of each person, getting into a brief encounter about God or faith, and being in awe of the beauty of the day. Along with being fed and feeding one another, the encounter includes the stuff of spirituality. It is all meaningful.

To me, the spiritual dimension in connections is not only vital but essential. And for us as the church, spirituality is at the heart of what we are and do.

Yet many times congregations need encouragement to delve into spiritual matters, to talk about their faith. How does one do that? Perhaps by starting meetings by asking questions such as "What has strengthened your faith?" and "What has challenged your faith?" and "Where have you sensed God's presence since we were last together?" Perhaps we should ask one another over and over again, "Why are you Christian?" until we all get to the heart of it. Or ask, "Who are the people who have been significant in your faith development? And why?" Listen attentively for respondent's own gifts coming through in how they respond.

Paying attention to one's spiritual life is an ongoing discipline. So is *being* the good news. It is up to the leadership team of the congregation to make sure that it happens within the congregation. Many visit a congregation hoping to find there someone who is living his or her faith. May yours be a congregation in which visitors encounter spiritual meaning and hospitality, where the welcome is tangible.

2

MAKING YOUR ENCOUNTERS COUNT

We hunger to be known and be understood. We hunger to be loved. We hunger to be at peace inside our own skins. We hunger not just to be fed these things but, often without realizing it, we hunger to feed others these things because they too are starving for them. We hunger not just to be loved but to love, not just to be forgiven but to forgive, not just to be known and understood for all the good times and bad times that for better for worse have made us who we are, but to know and understand each other to the same point of seeing that, in the last analysis, we all have the same good times, the same bad times, and that for that very reason there is no such thing in all the world as anyone who is really a stranger.

—FREDERICH BUECHNER[1]

THE ENCOUNTERS AT THE BREAD COUNTER ARE GENERALLY BRIEF AND quite short in comparison with the long rambling conversations I have with my friends. One way to look at this is that each time someone comes into the store, there is an opportunity to either connect or simply make a sale, to graciously welcome a customer or have a perfunctory exchange. It can be a pleasant contact with a product and money, or a cool, distant experience. An engagement can be personal and life giving, or it can seem life denying. Some of these bread store conversations have gone deeper and been satisfyingly connective. They have that transcending dimension. This is what an encounter can offer.

The word "encounter" means:

1. a meeting with a person or thing, especially a casual, unexpected, or brief meeting;
2. a meeting of persons or groups that are in conflict or opposition; combat, battle; and
3. an unpleasant situation.[2]

It is the first definition that applies to what I experience at the bread company. These brief encounters are chance meetings. Although coming into the store reveals that the customer intends to at least sample and/or buy something, the unexpected quality of connection may happen as well.

Another word that comes to mind as I reflect about the encounters at the counter is "serendipity," or unexpected surprise. Serendipity is:

1. the faculty or phenomenon of finding valuable or agreeable things not sought for;
2. an aptitude for making desirable discoveries by accident;
3. good luck in making unexpected and fortunate discoveries; and
4. the lucky tendency to find interesting or valuable things by chance.[3]

I see many customers who experience serendipity as they come into the store. Even though the encounters may be brief, the customer can find valuable things in unexpected places and people! That is not only because of the high quality of the bread and products that are totally expected, but also because of the unexpected benefit of the encounter with the staff. The way the encounters unfold is unplanned. The conversations are open-ended yet brief, and they may lead to serendipitous experiences, for both the customer and staff.

ENCOUNTERS ARE BRIEF

An average encounter with a customer takes two and a half to three minutes. That includes the hello, the naming of the bread samples, choosing the bread or other item, buying with cash or credit card, and then saying goodbye. So when does the spark occur that transforms this business transaction into a meaningful encounter? It may be the smile in the voice, or just the smile and the hello. It may be the tone of the voice, the eye contact with each other, or the open body posture. Or it could be something quite different: The words on the tee shirt or hat, the pin on the blouse or jacket, the boots, or the words on the sweatshirt or coat: any of these things may open the space for that encounter to occur between the staff and the customer.

Just in one morning, I had these encounters at the bread counter: a young woman said she was in training for a marathon in New Hampshire in four months; a former nurse shared that she had worked in the same hospital where I was a resident chaplain and had been a missionary nurse in South America where she became so burned-out that now she was working at Starbucks; a graduate student in film told me the plot of his movie project; another graduate student shared that he was studying counseling at a Buddhist university; the high school basketball team came in on its way to practice; the local university track team shared that they were ranked first in the Big Twelve; and a retired couple from a small town in the local hills came to sit at the counter to have coffee and a free slice of bread. All of these people came in for a brief time.

My almost ninety-year-old mother, when I told her about such brief encounters at the bread company said, "Short and sweet, dear. It's better than long, drawn out, and boring." She had been a stand-up comedian during her eighties. Her timing was always impeccable.

CREATING THE ENCOUNTERS

A line from E. M. Forster says a lot in two words: "Only connect."[4]

Such encounters may be brief, but how does one start them? What is the best way to open the space for some real human contact?

Spiritual awareness helps us see beyond what is right in front of us. For example, seeing the words "Church Choir Camp" on a middle-schooler's tee shirt led me to ask whether she sings in her church's choir, then what she likes about the choir. Her naming particular songs she enjoys led to her affirming her own faith through the music. The energy grew as the conversation expanded. Noticing, then asking an appropriate question, and then building on the answer with other questions can open the multilayered possibilities of a personal encounter.

A practice described by Danny Meyer, the entrepreneurial restaurant owner, hones his capacity to see what is going on around him in his restaurants that then leads to ways to engage people. He writes, "Making my rounds in the dining rooms involves, more than anything else, my ability to see, hear, and sense what's going on so that I can connect intelligently with our staff and guests and make things happen. I don't have a standard approach for every table, but I often start with a gut sense that a patron is ready for a visit."[5] Although the "gut sense" in reaching out to members and visitors is something that is nigh impossible to train, we can acknowledge it, hone it, practice it, and celebrate it, something that can be done in an informal conversation with others.

The following three encounters at the counter underscore what it means to pay attention, to see, and then to engage—in these cases, with a customer. A young man came into the store one morning and his tee shirt had the word "Anima" on it. I asked him if he knew what that meant. He didn't. "Do you know who C. J. Jung is?" I tried. "Yes," he said. "Well, the anim*a* is the feminine inner personality in the unconscious of a male, and the anim*us* is the unconscious of the female expressed as a masculine inner personality.[6] It is a way Jung understood our unconscious." As he left he said, "I will now prize my shirt even more."

A young woman entered one morning when there were not many customers and I asked how the day was going for her. "Fine, how about you?" she asked. "I am fine today for many reasons." I paused to see if she was going to pick up on my phrase. In one of those playful moods, I gestured with my hands as if I were asking her to ask me what at least one of the reasons would be. She finally picked up on my cue and asked, "Why?" Then I told her that I was working on a book about my encounters at the counter, and if she had not asked me a question, the conversation would have been even shorter. We would not have been having a conversation at all. I had to draw her out so that we could talk, even though it then resulted in about a five-minute conversation. It does take work to engage. And in order to have connection, there must be some effort.

A man came in wearing a parka, gloves, and hat although it was not that cold outside. I asked him why. He said his office was so cold he needed them. "Where is your office?" I asked. His office was in the local university where, I learned, he is a professor. He said he had taught in the east and the Midwest, and now here. When I asked where in the east, he mentioned Williamstown, Massachusetts. "You mean where Williams College is?" I asked. "Yes." "That is where William Sloane Coffin was a chaplain many years ago. Is that a name you know?" I asked. "Yes," he said. That very day I had been reading Coffin's book *Letters to a Young Doubter*, and a quotation came to me: "in a world of pain God is anything but immune from it."[7] Obviously, I am not always right on the mark. My questions led more to my recollecting particulars of Coffin's book than it did to uncovering more about the man in the interaction. The connection with this young professor brought to mind the wisdom of Coffin but it did not make a connection with the professor. My mind was not clear enough at that moment to listen to what the customer was saying.

There is a story about a student who had likewise come to a teacher filled with thoughts. The teacher began by asking the student to sit down and hold a teacup. As the teacher poured more and more tea into the student's cup, it began to overflow more and more. To the student's protests the teacher explained that the student had come already filled up and needed to be empty in order to learn. The message to me and to each of us who have many ideas and thoughts whirring in our minds is to be quiet and make room for the encounter to happen. Being full up precludes space for new experiences.

What do we need in order for a conversation to develop? First, there needs to be time, and even brief moments can be enough.

Second, the customer service staff really has to be present to the customer. There might be noise and bustle around, but it is possible to look directly at the customer and, holding your body still, be attentive to him or her. Third, there might be a visible clue about something to mention, as, for instance, the teenager's shirt with the words "Church Choir Camp" on it and the man who had on a Nebraska jacket. I could have decided not to mention either of these, but they were entry points for a conversation, ingredients for an encounter that did yield a connection. Fourth, we need to listen to what the customer is saying as well as what the customer is not saying, and notice what the customer is looking at.

People not only look different from each other; they *are* different from each other. Therefore, make your approach to each of them different too. One size does not fit all. Looking at a person's face, dress, and demeanor will tell you something about the person before you, but adding the tone of their voice and the way they respond to your approach to them tells even more. Communication is verbal and nonverbal. One study at UCLA indicated that up to 93 percent of communication effectiveness is determined by nonverbal cues. Another study indicated that the impact of a performance was determined by 7 percent of the words used, 38 percent by voice quality, and 55 percent by the nonverbal communication.[8] If there is an opportunity to ask a question, even more is revealed. It is important to see each situation as unique, just as the person is. Picking up on these clues makes for a unique encounter and for a memorable experience.

There are ways to have an innovative approach to customers. I find that new phrases and comments about the weather always lead to something if you stay with it. "Sunny and warm, but they say it will rain or even snow tomorrow." "Do you like any kind of weather?" I ask. "How's the day going for you?" Listening to their response can lead to conversation. A guy's shirt had a tree embroidered on it and I learned that he trims trees. He was up in a tree that morning. "Do you wear spikes?" I asked. "Only if the tree is dead, and I'm taking it down. Otherwise the spikes can injure a healthy tree." I had not considered that.

There are many ways to begin a conversation. John is a faculty member of the local university whom I knew from our congregation. I told him that several students had come in, and, when I had learned that they were in the Engineering Department, I had mentioned his name. He was not surprised; he had taught in and had also been in the administrative side of that department. As I reflected on that encounter, I realized that I had pigeonholed him just by his work role. I could just have readily begun our conversation by asking him about his kids or what he was looking forward to in the upcoming holiday. But I had focused on his title and that the students had known of him. In fact, I did not even recall the students' names so I could not make that connection. It felt as if I was objectifying him just because of his work. A reminder like this can help me redirect an encounter and make it more connecting.

I noticed the ring on the wedding finger of a young man who was there with a woman. I asked him about the ring. "That is a unique ring. Does it have particular significance?" "Yes," he said, "it is my engagement ring. My fiancée made hers and mine. The brown beads are exchanged for the white ones depending on how long we have been together. One white one for each year." There were three white ones. "What will you do when you get married?" I asked. "I will come up with something else," she said. One of the next times they came in, I saw that there were now four white beads on his ring. "How's it going?" I asked. "We are getting married," he said. "Hurrah," I said. I would not have had that moment of celebration with them if I had not noticed the rings before and asked about them, and then remembered it when I saw them the next time.

Sometimes as a way of noticing the person in front of me I try to guess what kind of bread a customer might want to try. I have said, "Here, this is the one you want to try." Sometimes I am right. Sometimes not. "Had the Apple Crunch?" I ask. "You want the Sunflower Wheat while we also have the Pecan Swirl out?" Without judgment, of course, I try to open a crack in the exchange in order to connect. Sometimes I act on assumptions just to get a reaction. Sometimes I give them an unusually large piece of bread—or even two!—to sample because they seem hungry. It all depends on what's happening in the interaction.

For connections to happen, we need to nurture the web of relationships. In the business setting, it is good to introduce people to each other who might have common interests and concerns. So also in a congregation. As people enter the store or as they come into a congregation, it can be helpful for each of them to look around and get a lay of the land. They might not yet want to share what it was that brought them into the store or to the congregation. However, after a time of introductions and getting acquainted, it might be appropriate to connect this person with others close by. Especially in a congregation it is very important to help a visitor make the acquaintance of a few other people with similar interests. And even if there do not appear to be any similarities between them, you never know what might emerge in connecting people with each other.

Robert came into the store when a couple of members of our congregation happened to be there as well. I introduced them since I knew Robert was from New Orleans. We had just had a fund raiser for Habitat for Humanity in New Orleans at our congregation. There is a constant flow of connections if you really pay attention to who people are and if you know even a bit about what is going in their lives.

If you are part of a congregation, I hope that you can translate these reflections into your context. I cannot give you magic steps for engaging in hospitality where you worship. Connections are human. They are not concocted to fit the encounter into a form you deem right. For the encounter to be real, the outcome is not programmed. This is true for how our congregations practice hospitality. "[H]ospitality is not a planned event," write Homan and Pratt, "or a series of routine gestures. It is the stance of the heart that is abandoned to Love."[9] In our congregation we plan where the visitor table is located, how many welcomers to have available to talk with visitors, what information to have available, when the next Exploring Membership gatherings will be, how often to invite the newer members to a luncheon to see how they are doing in becoming part of the congregation's life, and how we might use nametags in a helpful way. These are planned activities. However, if the "stance of the heart" is not open, loving, and spiritually vital, all of these activities will be like the "noisy gong or a clanging cymbal" described in 1 Corinthians 13:1. When the heart is open to love, there may even be a time of healing and hope in the encounter. We cannot make that happen, but we can be open to it. And to be open to it means we have the eyes of the heart to recognize that healing and hope are possible.

EXPERIENCING HEALING IN THE ENCOUNTERS

Another title that had come to me for this book was *Counter Therapy*. People come to the bread counter with their eyes on the bread board, which holds anywhere from three to eight different breads, muffins, scones, cookies, or brownies to sample. While it is ostensibly the bread that brings them in, I believe there is often another hunger that needs to be sated. I seek to engage them in conversation for as long as they are willing—provided that the line of customers behind them is not too long. Connecting has a therapeutic quality of healing. It is a way to discover pieces of experiences and then to put them together in a context of meaning.

In order for there to be an encounter, there needs to be engagement. Most of the engagements at the bread company are through words. It is a time of face-to-face experience without fear. It is time to offer an open space for speech. Nelle Morton wrote, "We empower one another by hearing the other to speech. We empower the disinherited, the outsider, as we are able to hear them name in their own way their own oppression and suffering. . . . Hearing in this sense can break through political and social structures and image a new system. A great ear at the heart of the universe—at the heart of our common life—hearing human beings to speech—to our own speech."[10] "Hearing human beings to speech." I love that. Creating a space so that a person can be heard may bring the balm of healing. We may not know for what a person needs healing, yet the offer of hearing may lead to an intimation of the brokenness that can receive some salve. In many of the stories that follow, there are seeds of healing that have been planted just by allowing the encounter to include listening.

One of the great gifts we can offer to each other is a listening heart. It is not about listening in order to disagree and rebut, or to get one's own story out, or to universalize the other's comments. It is about being able to listen with empathy and to hold the space for a person to feel truly heard, understood, and be known in their particularity. When listening comes from the heart, the setting is ready for an authentic encounter and for the possibility of healing.

In her book, *Too Late to Die Young*, Harriet McBryde Johnson gives a strong voice to a perspective that is unusual. Born with a disability, through her stories and her witness she teaches those who engage with the public about confronting "the life-killing stereotype that says we're all about suffering. We need to bear witness to our pleasures." She writes, "the widespread assumption that disability means suffering feeds a fear of difference and a social order that doesn't know what to do with those if it can't make us fit into its idea of normal." The healing comes, she says, as the gap between normal and not normal closes in to see all of us as human beings, engaged in "social engagement of all kinds: swapping stories, arguing hard, getting and giving a listening ear. . . . I enjoy those pleasures the same way nondisabled people do. There's no impairment; disability makes no difference."[11] In her humorous and challenging stories she offers us a way to find healing as we engage with those who might make some of us uncomfortable. It means having that "listening ear." Her book is a clarion call to expand and deepen the hospitality that we can offer.

Hospitality is a two-way street. Those who see themselves in the encounter on the giving side of hospitality, as at the bread counter, can learn receiving from the customer. Persons who are physically disabled can be the hosts for others, as Johnson's book underscores. The customer who came to the counter in his wheelchair invited the staff to come out from behind the counter and assist him in selecting bread. He told stories and amused the staff. His was a presence that welcomed us to interact in different ways. Another customer who is not able to talk comes in and gestures by way of communicating. It allows the staff to engage in movements and expressions that are unusual. Like the bread store staff, congregations that are learning about how to be accessible to all are invited to experience ways that they can welcome differently abled persons into the congregation. It means providing ways in the facilities as well as in the programs so that everyone can be in a welcoming space for the encounter to happen.

Along with the facilities and the programs, being hospitable also means opening the space within ourselves to be able to receive the gifts of others. I learned this as a hospital chaplain in the Butterfly Program, for children and their families in the hospital who are facing life-limiting illnesses. I had to learn that the heart that is accessible is a hospitable heart. Because of my encounters with those children and their families, I wrote an article called "When Listening Also Hurts!" Those connections taught me that "carving that space in one's own spirit and heart to make room for another takes time. It takes many times of coming to the end of the rope with people who do not know how to take the next step. It means stilling the traffic and chatter of one's own mind and heart in order to listen. And, the listening also does hurt. Without the defenses of explanation, verbal comforts, or distance, authentic listening can offer a deeper connection with the other person at their point of powerlessness."[12]

Attentiveness may bring forth that which is latent—humorous, touching, hopeful, simple, or even healing. There is an inevitable brokenness that comes to most of us if we live long enough. It may come through illness and disease, the failure or loss of relationships, losing a job, or suffering an injury that prevents us from doing something to which we are accustomed. An encounter may open up this hurt to a welcoming space in which the balm of a listening connection may happen.

Some stories that I have heard at the bread counter are of painful situations that have elicited tears. In the Gospel of Thomas we read, "If you bring forth that which is within you, what you bring forth will heal you. If you do not bring forth that which is within you, what you do not bring forth will destroy you."[13] The encounters at the counter can bring a connection that may lead to a wholeness that was not present when the customer came into the store.

Sometimes there is a choice to be made. Will you skirt what might be difficult to face, or will you welcome whatever is said?

Compassion allows you to face what is difficult. This is true in a business transaction just as it is in a congregation's hospitality. Nouwen writes that the word compassion "comes from the roots that mean literally to 'suffer with'; to show compassion means sharing in the suffering 'passion' of another. . . . To live with compassion means to enter others' dark moments. It is to walk into places of pain, not to flinch or look away when another agonizes. It means to stay where people suffer. Compassion holds us back from quick, eager explanations when tragedy meets someone we know or love."[14] True hospitality requires staff and congregants alike to be prepared to listen deeply. When this happens, hospitality is apparent.

I encountered such a dark moment of pain one February when our bread of the month was chocolate cherry in honor of Valentine's Day. An older woman came in who did not look very pleased. I could see it in her posture, the way she walked, and the way she looked up as I greeted her. In my usual way of trying to connect, I said, "This is the bread for St. Valentine's day. He was a saint who himself was killed because of an unfortunate situation. It was not a pretty story." I was thinking I might fill in more of the details to that situation when she said, "Well, my love is buried six feet under." "You are a widow?" I asked. "Yes, for twenty-eight years!" "Must be hard," I said. "It is hell," she responded. "I wanted to die before him. But what can you do?" I wondered if bringing that pain and sorrow out that quickly in that context was more painful than healing. Here at the counter this woman brought forth the experience that was still very raw and was present in her after so many years. However, I believe that bringing it into speech may lead to a renewing connection and a time, even a moment, for healing. I hope that she left feeling that the acknowledgement of her loss alleviated the hurt even a bit because a fellow human being had listened to it.

One of the members of my congregation came into the store. She and I had participated in a program sponsored by the National Association of Mental Illness (NAMI), called "Family to Family." Each of us has a family member with a brain disorder. In the twelve-week program, we learned and shared about the variety of mental illnesses, such as bipolar, anxiety, obsessive-compulsive, and schizoaffective disorders, along with schizophrenia and depression, which are all brain disorders. "Do you think my daughter could work here?" she asked. "She needs some work but she cannot work for more than several hours at a time." "How would she work with the high stresses, or the fast-paced business here?" I asked. "Well, she can be very critical. And she is very judgmental." Reflecting for a moment, I said, "It does not seem that this would be a good place for her." "I am beside myself sometimes," she said. "I don't know what she can do." "Is she taking her medications?" "She is not consistent." "Have you talked with the people we met in the NAMI program?" "Well, I have called but they do not have any recommendations for therapists or work situations." We left it that way. I continue to think about her and her daughter. What could be done?

One of the burdens I carry is that I think I can fix things all the time—or at least that I ought to be able to—by giving advice, making suggestions, and finding solutions. Such attempts at fixing are usually not very well received, however. It does not make for a genuine connection with a person. While I might have pursued some avenues to help this congregant's daughter, what was needed, I believe, was for her to name the struggle with which she was living with her daughter. Although it is painful, it is important to know that being in a place of powerlessness and feeling inadequate is real and human. Receiving that realization can deepen compassion as well as offer comfort. For many people who do have a loved one who is dealing with a mental illness or an addiction over which the family or friend has no control, such groups as NAMI or Al-Anon are very helpful. One of my favorite biblical verses is 2 Corinthians 12:9: "My grace is sufficient for you, for my power is made perfect in weakness." Paul was referring to Christ's grace and Christ's power being sufficient. It is our weakness and not our power that shows Christ's power. It is well for church staff and congregants to have a sufficiently strong spiritual foundation so that they embrace rather than be embarrassed by those times when no suggestion, advice, or solution is possible, let alone helpful. The help is in being helpless. Then, miracle of miracles, I have experienced that positive energy comes as the wind comes—from somewhere. In the movie *Doubt*, in his last sermon as he is leaving the parish, Father Flynn says, "there is a wind behind each of us that takes us through our lives. We never see it and we can't command it. We don't even know its purpose. (Yet) the wind that propels us is a superior knowledge. That is my faith." For me that wind beyond my control can bring me to new places and can offer new opportunities of healing and hope. Beyond my understanding, this divine energy can guide and lead me as long as I stay receptive to its presence.

A poem by Adrienne Rich speaks to the compelling passion of healing and our capacity to side with those who live for wholeness.

> *My heart is moved by all I cannot save:*
> *so much has been destroyed*
>
> *I have to cast my lot with those*
> *who, age after age, perversely,*
>
> *with no extraordinary power,*
> *reconstitute the world.*
>
> *A passion to make, and make again*
> *where such un-making reigns.*[15]

During the workday, the only time the staff at the bread company has to themselves is their thirty-minute lunch break. I make a sandwich, reflect on the encounters that morning, and read. One day, sitting a couple seats away at the lunch counter, an elderly man asked what I was reading. "It is about the experiences that people have had when their life has fallen apart," I replied, "when their dreams have been broken." "That's the kind of book I read," he said. He continued to talk throughout my entire lunch break. I did not need to say much but a "yes" here or there to keep him going. He was a security guard but wanted to be an architect. "I didn't have the money for school," he said. "You know," he continued, "the Bible has a lot about herbs. And the Chinese, they knew about herbs." The disjointed conversation continued about his children, his wife, his reading. My eyes glazed over. It is not always possible to be totally present and really listen. I try but don't always succeed. I did not open my book again during that lunch break. I don't know what he needed, but I hope that in telling his story he received a modicum of healing.

Sometimes it is I who receive, from the customer. This customer's hat gave him away. "Jamaica." It was a bike-racing hat, not a helmet. "Did you see *Cool Runnings*?" I asked. "Yes." "Been to Jamaica?" "Yes. Just came back." "Why did you go?" "It was a vacation. My kidneys have failed and I just needed to go somewhere other than here." "When did that happen?" "A couple years ago." "Did your time in Jamaica help?" "For a while, I guess. Now I am back. It was difficult being there since kids came to me all the time asking for money. People are poor." "Quite a different perspective," I responded. Was his own physical limitation a context in which he could empathize with others? The poor condition of his kidneys mirrored the poverty of the children. With the bread I gave him, he fed me the reality of many people's human condition and his courage in living with his.

Around 3:30 P.M. that same day, I asked a young woman how her day had been. "Well," she said, "It started quite strange. Right in the middle of the worst snowstorm we have yet had this winter, I ran out of gas on the highway. I was just able to pull over so I got out of my car and hitchhiked to get gas. People were wonderful. I got back and as I was putting the gas in the car, I noticed there were two large snowplows stopped behind me. I rushed as much as I could. I knew I was inconveniencing people. Then I got the car going and, well, here I am. Thanks for asking and giving me a chance to tell my story."

You could say this was a fairly innocuous conversation, but we can all remember ones in which we felt uncomfortable by how much anxiety or relief or pain a person was disclosing to us. Nouwen writes, "In so many encounters we try to look away from the pain. We try to help our friends quickly process grief. . . . All the while, however, we act less out of genuine 'suffering with' and more out of our need to stand back from the discomfort we might feel. . . . One reason we respond to others this way is because we are skirting our own pain. We resist getting near the suffering of another partly out of our unwillingness to suffer ourselves."[16]

Later we consider how customer service and congregational ministry of hospitality training might nurture this capacity to be empathetic. For now, I pause to underscore that the encounters in business *may* include these healing and spiritual dimensions and to respond to the concern that asking customer service staff to focus on this aspect of their work may seem a bit unrealistic or be asking too much. In reality I believe being aware of this quality in the encounters in business must not be overlooked. Perhaps paying attention to the possibility of healing in the encounter may be more appropriately done in our congregations, yet customer service staff does well at least to be aware of it.

Naturally, not all of our encounters can be deep and tap into those painful places that each of us carries daily. "Discretion requires you to respect someone without trying to be their best friend," write Homan and Pratt. "Hospitality is not a call to unquestioning intimacy with the whole world."[17] "Every relationship does *not* have to involve gut-level sharing. It is a beautiful thing to simply respond to others' everyday, simple needs."[18] As one who can become very earnest in my ministry of hospitality, hoping that I can get under the skin of everyone in each encounter, that is a helpful reminder. The reason angels can fly, some say, is because they take themselves lightly. Discerning when to approach an issue that may be painful, and when to be less probing, is a practice that is necessary to learn. It means engaging in conversations lightly, too. Bringing yourself to every situation with an open heart will usually lead to the most appropriate way to offer hospitality, a hospitality that is genuine and honest.

The occasions that provide a context in which an encounter can occur and in which healing may happen include the unexpected as well as the anticipated. In my work in hospitals, while patients and their families are not glad to be there other than because they are seeking healing and relief for their suffering, it is my hope that healing may come in the encounter. I even anticipate it. However, when the grace of healing does not come, it may not be because of my intended purpose to be present or even because of what I do or say. There are just those times when there is nothing that can be done or said that would seem to precipitate even a moment of healing. Those are those occasions when the depth of grief or the experience of powerlessness is excruciatingly tangible. On the other hand, in the setting of the bread company more often I find it to be a refuge and a re-energizer. While I came into the store with a bounce in my step, I have come to realize that there are unexpected times when the same pain and sorrows are present there as they are in the hospital setting, and as they are in the congregational setting. As many of the stories that I have heard and shared at the bread company show, not everyone who comes into the store is deeply happy in his or her life situation. If you just scratch the surface of almost anyone's life, you will find pain, suffering, and trouble. Awareness of this human condition leads not only to empathy but also to a capacity to listen more deeply wherever you are.

Since the bread store is located in the town in which I have been living for more than eight years, many people came in whom I already knew but who were surprised to see me in an apron at the bread counter. Tim, a dad of a young man who had a brain tumor and is now a cancer survivor, remembered me from their time at the hospital when I was chaplain. He came in for some bread after his son was through with treatment and was in recovery. Seeing me, Tim asked, "What are you doing here? It sure is a different setting for you." While I was at the hospital, my way of being was by listening, encouraging, and being present, realizing the high level of anxiety for him and his family, as well as for his son. There was not actually a lot for me to do. The child life staff, the social worker, the nursing staff, and the doctors all offered tangible ways to support this family. I found myself talking to the dad quite a bit. More than doing for him, I was just being with him.

Tim struggled with his own spirituality and his pursuit of knowledge about the cancerous tumor. Because of the months of treatment at the hospital and the follow-up, Tim asked to visit the oncology unit to share his experiences with other parents who were also going through this very difficult time. He came to our parent lunches several times before we asked if he wanted to do more volunteer work. As a result, he went through the volunteer training program at the hospital so that he could play his guitar to groups at the hospital. All of this came out as we talked with each other over the counter.

"Are you still playing music at the hospital for the kids?" I asked Tim when I saw him the next time at the store. "Yes, every other week. There are patient situations that break your heart. I think the music gives them a break even if it is for just a few minutes. It offers an experience that is new and different for them. In fact, the parents sometimes break down. Some cry. They like the '60s music I play. They can relate." Since his own son has recovered, his compassion now comes from being a parent of a child with cancer.

Sometimes there is no opportunity to see the results of the "work" that one does, especially for chaplains with their patients. It was fortifying to visit with Tim and hear of the progress of his son. It was also confirming to hear of Tim's venture into his volunteer work resulting from his experience. His "ministry of music" was developed by his experience at the hospital. At the bread counter, he affirmed the gifts that have come to him through his trials. It was a follow-up, right there.

Such stories demonstrate that the infusion of spirituality into the encounters gives a quality of connection that may be healing. This can be as true at the bread company as in the congregation, as long as the encounter is authentic and we are not engaging the other out of our own neediness or using the other as the means to our own ends. "Healing encounters and deep communion with others come about from persons who have experienced at least a taste of love offering love to another, without manipulation or subtle games."[19]

As spirituality laces those settings of obvious suffering and pain as well as those less noticeable settings of hardship and struggle, healing is also grounded in the simple things. The work at the bread counter encompasses small and ordinary things, like slicing bread, talking about the breads available, or making a latte. Newman talks about hospitality as a practice of the "little way," a phrase made famous by St. Therese of Lisieux. "God takes the little things we are capable of and transforms them. Waiting for the great opportunity or the path to success can blind us to our daily reliance upon God's bread and the ordinary ways we can give this bread to others."[20] I like this quotation because for me the word "bread" points to both the spiritual food and the actual bread. Both combine in the way that the bread is offered and in the way the bread is received. In these little things, the larger meaning comes. In the ordinary, the extraordinary can come.

The goal of being present to others by being hospitable is not to make the staff or the members of a congregation perfect. That is not realistic. However, helping us become aware of their and our own imperfection and embracing that allows the encounter to deepen, so there is a possibility for healing and hope. Nouwen talks about the everlasting love, the first love, and the all-embracing love of God that is the foundation for being detached enough to be present. "Your love for others can be unconditional, without a condition that your needs are gratified, when you have the experience of being loved."[21] People who experience this love "radiated a certain inner freedom. They made me aware that they were in touch with more than themselves. They pointed to a reality greater than themselves from which and in whom their freedom grew. This centeredness, this inner freedom, this spiritual independence had a mysterious contagiousness."[22] When this contagion grows, the whole environment vibrates with energy and life. The affirmation of faith in this first love of God is spoken about in our congregations. Paul Tillich wrote a sermon that includes this now classic statement: "You are accepted. . . . Simply accept that you are accepted." Simple to say, difficult to embrace. Yet it is the invitation in most congregations weekly, and the reason it is usually weekly is because most of us find it too difficult to accept our acceptance. We have to be reminded of it over and over.

As I have been exploring the healing dimensions in our encounters in the store and in our congregations, it is important to highlight the expectations of those who are in customer service as well as those in our ministry of hospitality. Having clarity of the mission and purpose of the encounter need not make the conversation static or formulaic but rather can provide a framework in which hospitality can expand.

CLARIFYING ONE'S EXPECTATIONS AND MISSION

What is the intention of the customer service staff? To sell? To connect? Both? Perhaps the highest priority of the staff person is helping the customer feel better when they leave than when they came into the store. What would that mean?

Almost everyone who comes into the store is aware of the offer of a free slice of bread with butter and honey. That is the trademark of this store. It is a relished routine for the regular customers, and first-timers learn quickly. However, if the staff person's goal is to engage the customer, how can that happen?

When people come to the door, I ask myself, "What are they looking for? A free slice? A sandwich, or a loaf of bread?" I can track their eyes as they look at the breadboard, or at the shelves with the bread, or as they head for the sandwich making area. Meeting people at the counter is a little like trying to discover a mystery plot. Who are these people? What is their story today? What might lead us to conversation and connection? Be gentle, I remind myself, because I do not know what burdens and worries they are carrying this day, at this time. "Philo of Alexandria, a renowned Jewish scholar who lived at the beginning of the first millennium, once said, 'Be kind, for everyone you meet is fighting a great battle.'"[23] There are people like this young electrician who came in for a sandwich. He had confidence, chutzpah, and boldness. I joked with him and met him where his energy was. Very different than being with that quiet, subdued woman whose voice was just slightly over a whisper and who was very hesitant about which piece of bread to try. Each of them has a story, I know. I understand that there are inner struggles that each person is carrying that do not easily come to the surface. Therefore it is important to be expectant and welcoming, remaining open to the unfolding mystery.

For connections to happen, it helps if the staff person is prepared. Being aware of what the customer is expecting and being open to what may be said shapes the staff person's expectation, too. To expect an encounter that is real and genuine is something that the staff person can keep in the forefront of his or her mind. There are also some ways to get ready before work begins. It might be by a brief intake of breath, then letting the breath go through you, centering and relaxing you. That is a good practice between sales as well. Taking a sip of water adjusts my attitude and demeanor. Although I do not believe that we can *make* the encounter spiritually vital, it does help if we are in tune with our self and in tune with the energy of life. It will allow the space needed for an encounter that is more than a transaction to happen. It *may* then become a spiritual encounter.

And it may not. For that I have to be prepared too. As Peter Gomes, chaplain at Harvard University, said in one of his sermons, "Get over it. Get used to it. Get on with it." When there is a customer whom I have not satisfied, I need to let it go. The man who was gruff because I could not hear him, or the man who grabbed his bread and went off in a huff when I said that all I needed was some more change to pay for the bread—those two situations stuck in my craw. It takes time to let sink in what has happened. It may take more than several moments to mull it over it, to be self-reflective about what just happened. Then, I may *get over it.* I understand that there are things going on in most people's lives that have absolutely nothing to do with me, so I can *get used to it.* There will be more people to serve, so I can then *get on with it.* These three phrases of Gomes's are helpful in understanding those awkward moments. Knowing that each encounter can be an adventure, I need not be intimidated but rather can be fascinated, attentive, and then move on.

I once read that Eleanor Roosevelt said if you approach each new person you meet in the spirit of adventure, you will find yourself endlessly fascinated. We had been in one of the longest periods of having snow on the ground in Boulder. We had three blizzards and five weekends of snow. That is unusual given that snow here usually melts after only a couple of days. A woman came in and was a bit grumpy about how much snow we were having. I was wondering what her story might be. What was my expectation in this encounter? To listen? To respond right back with grumpiness? Or to engage in conversation with empathy? The time with this woman became an opportunity to talk about how we can choose what our attitude can be about whatever is happening to us. The snow could be seen as an adventure to explore or just something about which to complain. It is something that is out of our control. We had a ninety-second conversation that made us both appreciate having the time to look at the situation from more than one perspective. That was an adventure in itself and it confirmed the mission of customer service.

The phrase, "Keep the main thing the main thing," has been around for a while. It urges us to stay on point, keep the mission in front of us, have our eyes on the prize all the time, and keep our focus. The Great Harvest Bread Company's main thing—their mission—is to sell bread. Providing good customer service is the way to accomplish that mission. Along with that focused mission of selling bread, the way in which the bread is sold is part of the mission as well. The means and the end are conjoined. That the customer is pleased in the encounter and that she has the bread she wants both embody the mission.

As I offered the standard free slice of bread, asking a customer what her bread choices would be, she said, "I bet it is great working here." "Why?" I asked. "Because you please the customer." The panoply of bread choices we offer a customer, the leeway that we have to offer a taste of anything, the freedom to respond to a customer's need beyond their expectation, and having a smile in the voice and the direct eye contact all added up to "pleasing customers," at least for this one woman! Meyer puts it this way, "hospitality starts with the genuine enjoyment of doing something well for the purpose of bringing pleasure to other people. Whether that's an attitude, a behavior, or an innate trait, it should become a primary motivation for coming to work every day."[24]

In the context of a congregation, in particular in a Christian situation, a church's mission might be summarized in the words of H. Richard Niebuhr. "The purpose of the church is to increase the love of God and neighbor."[25] Congregations do this by embodying the good news in which we say we believe by welcoming people into God's realm. Congregations show forth who God is by how they welcome one another. The three ingredients that our local church is weaving into a new mission statement are transforming spirituality, radical inclusion, and compassionate service. As our church seeks to embody these foci, our church becomes the mission!

3

MAKING HOSPITALITY COME ALIVE

*To practice hospitality in our world, it may be
necessary to evaluate all the laws and all the
promotions and all the invitation lists of corporate and political society from the point of the
view of the people who never make the lists.
Then hospitality may demand that we work to
change things.*

—JOAN CHITTISTER[1]

WHAT IS THE GOAL OF A CONGREGATION'S HOSPITALITY? THE SPIRIT OF
welcome in all of its manifestations is at the heart of hospitality. As
congregations practice hospitality, God's presence is being acknowledged and people are being welcomed.

In her powerful, fictional short story entitled "The Welcome
Table," Alice Walker tells us about a congregation's lack of welcome.
An older black woman is thrown out of a white Christian congregation in the south as she enters. Then she is welcomed by Jesus as they
walk and almost skip down the highway together. Walker evokes the

painful experience of rejection as well as the blissful welcome of the Divine. In the *Guide to Reflection*, the editors of that short story collection ask, "Think about your own congregation. Is it a place where 'misfits' are welcome? What makes a 'misfit' anyway?"[2] The experience of hospitality in a congregation is a reflection of how the sacred is lived out. It is communal. It is social. It is observable. From the perspective of the outsider or the "misfit," we learn what the measure and the quality of welcome are, as well as the depth of the spirituality in a particular congregation.

So as we prepare our hearts, spirits, and spaces to receive people into our congregation, we need to have eyes to help create an experience that is welcoming. It may mean putting yourself in the place of those who are coming to the services or offering a program (such as child care) in order to provide what is necessary to assist in the welcome. The congregation in Alice Walker's story did not offer any comfort or assurance to the woman who sought to enter. What was her life like? What was she seeking? Who was she? Instead of finding out, simply on the basis of her race they decided that she didn't fit in there. In our congregations, we are to make space for everyone. "The image of preparing a table, or preparing a place, is a good overall image for hospitality. In genuine hospitality we work to make our entire existence a welcoming table, a place prepared for others to be at ease, to receive from us comfort and strength," Homan and Pratt remind us.[3]

The root words of hospitality are "love of stranger." In many contexts when persons seem to be outsiders or misfits, they are strangers. Xenophobia refers to the fear of strangers, but the congregation that is grounded in spiritual integrity is a place where there is a place at the table for the stranger. It is not our own selves who are the hosts at the table, but the One who is the host for all. Bringing the stranger to the table makes the stranger a person of value and worth right along with everyone else. Our hospitality demonstrates our love, a love that is offered when the place is prepared and the person is welcomed at the table. "The depth of our spirituality is measured by the degree of our hospitality" is an axiom I have carried with me over the years.

In the inspiring story of Zacchaeus recorded in Luke 19:1–10, there are at least five components that illustrate this hospitality:

1. *Zacchaeus had some sense of his need to see Jesus.* In spite of his own status as a person who was an outsider, he was drawn to see this One who was making a stir. Our need brings us to God.

2. *Zacchaeus was persistent.* Since he was not able to see over the crowd, rather than leaving, he climbed a tree to get a better view. It is not easy to "break into" already formed groups, including congregations! For the welcome to be truly embodied, it does take some persistence on the part of the visitor, along with the congregation's willingness to be open to the newcomer.

3. *Zacchaeus was acknowledged and affirmed by Jesus.* Jesus saw him in the tree and invited himself to be Zacchaeus' guest. Made invisible by the crowd and on the outskirts of the action, Jesus saw Zacchaeus as a person of value and worth and brought him right into the center of the action. Founded on the faith that one's value is based on God's loving acceptance of each of us, the hospitality in our congregations will have the quality of acknowledgement that invites everyone to come to the table.

4. *Zacchaeus "was happy to welcome" Jesus.* Zacchaeus became the host because Jesus had created a space for Zacchaeus to be who he really was. As congregations realize that God is the host and each person is welcome as he or she is, each person can welcome others.

5. *Zacchaeus gave generously.* He offered half of all his possessions to the poor. Who is the guest? Who is really the host? Zacchaeus and Jesus each lived both of those roles in this story. After being welcomed himself, Zacchaeus was no longer an outsider but was able first to welcome Jesus and subsequently to welcome others by sharing his riches. In our

congregations, because God has welcomed us so unconditionally, we are freed to live with gratitude and extend our gifts of welcome to the world.

In workshops I have asked members of a congregation to invite an "outsider"—that means someone who is not a member of the congregation—to attend a worship service with the intention that afterwards the "outsider" shares what their experience was like. This exercise is to help the congregation see itself from the perspective of someone who is not familiar with the patterns and habits of the congregation. How did the congregation embody the spirit of welcome? How did they thwart it? The hospitality team might come up with a list of areas about which the "outsider" might reflect. That might include parking, entering the facility, the welcome at the door, assistance in finding a seat, the clarity of the order or worship, whether the service was engaging, whether anyone talked with you after the service, when you received any information about the congregation's activities, whether you were invited to the Fellowship Time after the service, whether anyone introduced you to others, and whether you were invited to return. The hospitality team could make their own list that is appropriate to your congregation. Then the team could ask the "outsider" to sit with them and share his or her reflections. Just as it is futile to ask a fish what water is like, so too it is difficult to know what it is really like to attend your congregation unless you are actually a newcomer.

Many businesses use a "Mystery Shopper" program. A secret customer grades the business on a range of criteria, from friendliness to cleanliness. It's a good idea for the business. Likewise, in our congregations, it is helpful to have a person experience our worship or our programs, someone who has some understanding of what congregations are intending to communicate and offer. The "outsider" can be helpful to those who are in the congregation by being aware of the criteria that are appropriate for congregations and for that particular congregation.

Your hospitality team can also reflect on how they themselves have experienced that congregation's—or another's—hospitality. Simple suggestions might include making sure signs are clear and that there are directional signs toward the sanctuary, the childcare area, the elevator, or the restrooms. Is there a sign indicating an area where those wanting more information about the congregation and its programs would be able to find them? If so, is there a specific website address for people to know about the congregation's statement or covenants as well as the programs? In addition, is there someone there to respond to questions and engage in conversation? This is particularly important if the visitor has actually taken the effort to go to the fellowship time after the service. Many congregations have permanent nametags that they use during the fellowship time. Depending on the size of the congregation, the logistics of where to keep the nametags can become tricky. However it works, it is a sign of a gracious welcome to have nametags available so people can talk with one another by name!

I came across a review of a restaurant in Denver. The reviewer articulated the three top reasons, that he likes to go out to dinner: (3) to enjoy good food; (2) to spend time with friends; and (1) to revel in the restaurant's hospitality. In other words, if he likes a restaurant, it has more to do with the hospitality and the experience of being there than it does with the food. When I look at a congregation the way I look at my business experience, I see more clearly what the congregation needs to do to extend hospitality. As in the restaurant, so in the congregation, hospitality is at the top of the list.

The restaurant reviewer also commented about other ingredients that make for a memorable experience and what the lures are for returning. Those are the genuine atmosphere of welcoming that pervades the place, being greeted gregariously and appreciatively, and the feeling of being taken care of. These qualities can pervade any place of business where there is the possibility for an encounter between the customer and the customer service staff, as of course they can also be present in our congregations.

Meyer comments, "there is simply no point for me—or anyone on my staff—to work hard every day for the purpose of offering guests an average experience. I want to hear: 'We love your restaurant, we adore the food, but your people are what we treasure most about being here.'"[4] Meyer's book pays attention to the people who interact with the customer—the staff. Meyer encourages "each manager to take ten minutes a day to make three gestures that exceed expectations and take a special interest in our guests."[5] With this intention and attention to the guests, the managers themselves will be making hospitality come alive.

What would it look like for those called into the ministry of hospitality in your congregation to take just five minutes before they began their welcoming on Sunday morning to make the ministry of hospitality come alive? Here's my suggestion:

- One minute remembering the purpose of the congregation. This might be "to increase the love of God and neighbor." Whatever the "mission" of your congregation, it can also motivate your hospitality.

- Two minutes thinking about new people you have met previously at church and are getting to know.

- Two minutes visualizing the spirit of welcome that will come through your smile, your handshake, your voice, your open posture, and where you are standing as a welcomer.

Hospitality means creating a space in which the welcoming Spirit of the Holy is engaged in an encounter. This encompasses our attitude, the environment, acknowledgment of and listening to the other, our genuine concern for the other's well-being, and responding appropriately to the other's needs. Even the smile needs to be genuine, not a "smiley button" smile but one that comes from a genuine place of graciousness.

Michele Hershberger, in her book *A Christian View of Hospitality: Expecting Surprises*, invites people to do the "Forty-Day Experiment." People are to "Pray every day that God would send them a hospitality opportunity, record their experiences in a journal, and then send the journals to me."[6] The book is a compilation of those experiences interwoven with biblical stories. One of her own stories indicates that hospitality can be very difficult if not almost impossible. When her daughter was beaten up not once but twice at school, Michele had to face her own "hospitality opportunity" in meeting the one who had beaten up her daughter. It was fearful. It was fretful. And it was surprising. Yet the stories in the book do compel the reader to be hospitable by having spiritual eyes and therefore seeing how to welcome the stranger, seeing a "hospitality opportunity." We turn a blind eye to many such opportunities in our daily lives. To put that challenge front and center as we get on with our activities may change the way we see. Offering genuine hospitality in those places even when it makes one uncomfortable is a mark of the presence of God. It offers way more than a handshake and a smile! It comes from a transforming experience with the Holy. Yet, perhaps, the test of the degree of hospitality is in those situations where there is some fear and fret as well as some surprise.

Situations in which to extend hospitality can be difficult, as Hershberger's story reveals. Although such situations do not occur as much in business, the depth of welcome in a congregation can lead to places that are quite uncomfortable. In my congregation, when a man who is a member of our church and is autistic wanted to go on one of our mission trips to New Orleans, it presented a problem for some. There are some things about this man that are annoying. He has a need to hold a hand, to put his head on a person's shoulder, to touch someone's arm frequently, and he has no awareness of "personal" space. He has a sweet spirit. Although his voice is very loud and he understands everything people are saying, he talks in a group conversation in ways that do not follow the topic. Dialogues are minimal, although possible. It is immediately clear that he is "different."

At the counter in the bread company, there was no one who guarded the door. Everyone was let in. So it would seem to be the case at a congregation. Everyone is welcome, the church sign usually says. However, it is one thing to be open-minded and welcoming to those who are like us; it is another to welcome those who definitely are not. I remember the Rev. Jeremiah Wright once saying, "Different is not deficient. Different is different."

As one gets under the surface of hospitality in our congregations, we experience the welcome to those who are "different." Are they present in our worship services? Are they welcomed into the fellowship times of our church? Are they invited to share in the mission of our church? Are there accommodations or "sacrifices" that we must make to incorporate someone who has special needs? Are we realizing the gifts that these "different" people are bringing to our church? These are the questions that compel congregations to wrestle with the quality of their welcome. It is very easy to say that congregations are to be inclusive, but actually to be so in such a program as the mission trip in my church can be challenging.

One of the unintended results of highlighting hospitality might be in overdoing it. If the welcome is too effusive and the customer happens to be an introvert or is in a funk, the interaction might fall flat. If the welcome is not fitting or appropriate it might skew the encounter. In addition, always to be "up" as staff may lead to burnout. So when one's energy is flagging at the bread counter, how about switching tasks with a colleague? This might give one a different and fresh perspective—or of course it might simply detract from looking at what leads to the experience of burnout in the first place.

I have wondered about modulating the greeting I offer in order to be appropriate to where people are. There was a man who came into the store and there was no way that I could bring him out in spite of my cajoling and nudging him to try some bread, or see what a beautiful day it was, or what a funny face I was drawing on his bread card. He was just as he was. I expect that even if I had done a physical or verbal dance, he would not have responded. I challenged myself to connect and find a way to elicit some liveliness in the encounter. However, going overboard is not helpful either. In my approach, I do not want to be underwhelming, but neither do I want to be overwhelming. I would lean more toward the latter, though. I really like to hook the customer's attention. A smile, a genuine and authentic hello, not one that is robotic, and a welcoming demeanor say to the customer "I am open to you." This particular customer did not change from when he entered until he left. Sometimes all I have is the intention and the result falls flat. We can, however, stay awake all the time and hope that doing the best we can is really the best.

Jesus said, "Keep awake therefore."[7] Being awake and present does not mean that the content of the conversation is prescribed before the conversation even begins. There are people who daily carry heavy burdens, such as the woman I mentioned previously whose husband died many years ago. The gift in that conversation was that she was able to bring that grief into speech. Being awake to the possibility that a customer may be experiencing a job loss, or is depressed, or may even have experienced the death of a loved one, creates a space in your mind and heart to be attuned to such difficult situations. A phrase, a word, a gesture, or the physical bearing of the customer may be a trigger to you to pause and pay attention to what is going on. It may be that the situation is not spoken about out loud at first. However, if the customer service staff person does not do the perfunctory interaction, the customer just may open up and acknowledge what she or he is carrying. Dismissing the clues that are being shared thwarts the possibility of connection. Of course, many customers do not come to the store to unburden themselves, but some do, especially if their prior experience was welcoming and positive. The staff can even say, "How's it going?" and really listen! "What's happening?" can open up an affirmation of how things actually are. There does not need to be a thirty-minute conversation for even the brief acknowledgment of what is going on to be an affirmation that gives energy and life.

The overwhelming or the underwhelming hospitality along with the connection with those who are carrying burdens applies also to our congregations. The first encounter in our congregation is usually at the beginning of a worship service and is usually offered by the greeters. However, it is important to have welcomers as well, especially in congregations where there are generally visitors. The welcomers are front-line people whose hospitality means paying particular attention to those who have that sort of lost look, or who seem unsure of where to go and what to do. A good beginning is a simple, "Hello, my name is _____ . I don't think we have met before." This creates an opening. Many visitors are coming to check out the congregation but may not want twenty questions, preferring to come in quietly, experience the service, and then leave.

A question that is appropriate if there is time before or after the service is, "What brings you to our church today?" If the welcomer's mind and heart are open and alert, the response might give a clue of what visitors are looking for and what is going on in their lives. Responses might include, "We are looking for a church for our children," "We have just moved into town," "I have not been to a church for years and I felt it was time to try it again," or "I read about you on the church's website and I am looking for a church that is open and inclusive." Each of those responses opens doors for further conversation. That might happen during a fellowship time after the service where the visitor might appreciate the opportunity to learn more about the congregation and meet others. Or, they may not. The welcomer may also ask for the person's name, telephone number, and/or e-mail address, preferably using a form that is already prepared, and can ask if the person would like to have one of the church staff people give them a call. This is an especially helpful invitation if the welcomer senses that there is more going on in the person's life than the welcomer can deal with. The welcomer has to be responsive, not pushy nor over the top in the welcome. Being sensitive and contextual is important.

Even as the greeters and the welcomers are the first encounters that a visitor will have when they visit, gracious hospitality can nourish and nurture. The use of the words "nourish" and "nurture" in the same sentence brings together two foci that combine to make hospitality genuine. It is more clearly seen in the restaurant business, perhaps, but I know that it applies to the Great Harvest Bread Company, too. Meyer writes, "Guests may think they're dining out to feel nourished, but I've always believed that an even more primary need of diners is to be nurtured."[8] It is one thing to enjoy the deliciousness of the warm bread, and it is another is to be seen, known, and acknowledged. Both of these needs are important, although I believe the primacy of being in relationship makes the food even more palatable. In

Proverbs 15:17 we read, "Better is a dinner of vegetables where love is than a fatted ox and hatred with it." The food, yes, *and* the manner in which it is served.

This we can translate to our congregations. Members come to be nourished with the spiritual food of worship, education, fellowship, and mission. It is nourishing and it is nurturing. D. H. Lawrence writes in his poem "We Are Transmitters," that all of us do transmit life and when we hold onto life or hoard it, life does not flow.[9] We have been given the gift of life's energy, and giving it to others as well is at the core of what life is. However, this energy is not to be wasted or given away cheaply. It is to be given so that even more life can come forth.

The life that we transmit in our congregations is the life of faith. This faith is large enough to hold all of life—with its laughter and its tears. One gesture of hospitality we offer in my congregation is having tissues available in the pews. It signals that "there is room for all of your feelings here. You are welcome as you are." The whole of life, with its joys and its terrors, its fears and regrets and celebrations, is invited to be present. On several instances, I have had the occasion to offer a handkerchief to a person who was overcome with emotion before, during, or after worship. This simple act affirms that life's struggles are welcome here.

To engage with energy and to receive and give life at the bread company, the customer service staff's attitude and state of mind shape what happens in the exchange. As I said previously, what the customers are wearing and the words on their hat, sweatshirt, or tee shirt say something. They are clues or avenues in which an encounter can take shape. These many entrees for a conversation go beyond the cost of the bread and whether or not they can find their bread card or if they have one. Are they by themselves or do they have children? Are they part of a family or are they a couple, married or not? Reading these signs might open doors for contact with the person(s). When the staff is alert and attentive to the customer, they embody hospitality. The attitude of hopeful expectation creates room for hospitality.

Here are some practices I learned from my work at the bread store that we can easily apply in a congregational context:

1. *Acknowledge the person in front of you.* Seems simple, but it is not. While it might seem that the "agenda" at the store is to make the sale, the real basis of the interaction is a genuine and authentic connection with the person who is right there with you. It means consciously making space for the encounter physically, mentally, spiritually, and emotionally.

2. *Be attentive to what you see and hear, as well as what you do not see or hear,* as you engage with the person. What does the customer's tone of voice, facial expression, body posture, or sweatshirt tell you?

3. *Listen.* Be quiet enough so that the person can say what it is that she or he wants to say—about the product or service they need, or about life in general.

4. *Bring zest into the connection by changing things up a little.* Rather than always saying "Good morning," or "Have a good day," how about "Hope your afternoon is wonderful" or "How's the day treating you and how are you treating the day?"

5. *Follow up on clues so the conversation can go somewhere.* Draw your customer out if he or she seems willing, and if not, then keep to a quick and polite business transaction.

We can learn these practices and still encounter others' reticence to our approaches. There are at least these reasons for such reticence: First, a congregation member withholds reaching out to someone because of not knowing for sure if the person is a visitor or a member. To counter this dilemma, I suggest that one of the questions *not* to use is, "Are you visiting?" because it might be they are a member but have not been around for a long time or they are unfamiliar to you because the congregation is too large for you to know everyone who is a member. A better greeting, as I mentioned previously, is: "Hello, I am _____ and I don't think we have met before." That gets the conversation going. Second, people resist meeting new people because they don't want to be embarrassed. Third, some people are reticent because they may know the other person but have momentarily forgotten their name or even what their prior conversation was all about! Directness is the best policy on this one. You can say, "Please remind me of your name, I have forgotten." Or, "I am Alan, please tell me your name again." The other person will appreciate your own humility on this score because it will help make the connection rather than missing the chance for hospitality to happen.

There are other reasons why it is important to reach out to those that you do not know in the first place as well those who are known to you. First, as a member of the congregation you are representing the good news of the congregation. Your own faith affirms that each person is unique and valued in the eyes of God. You can make that faith tangible by your welcome. Second, you have the adventure of getting to know someone you did not know before. The gifts and interests that the other has will be engaging and intriguing. Third, the visitor has come to worship for specific reasons and you may be the one who helps that person find something for which he or she is looking. The good news continues to be good news as you reconnect with each other. The gifts and interests of one another can be underscored. And life has happened since you met the last time and the worship this day may have particular resonance in the other. You will never know if you do not overcome your reticence.

Another way in which the hospitality of the congregation can develop and grow is by the way in which connections are made through the worship service itself. When the relationships between people and God and people with others are underscored, even the greeters and the welcomers may catch that emphasis of genuine connection, and they can pass it along. The themes of worship services and even the stories that are shared in the worship and names mentioned in the prayers can create a level of comfort that allows people to share their own stories and thereby be connected. "There is no stronger way to build relationships than taking a genuine interest in other human beings and allowing them to share their stories," writes Meyer.[10] In my congregation, two of the most significant services during the year are Gratitude Sunday and Open and Affirming Sunday. Both of them involve telling stories and both of them have augmented the atmosphere of hospitality to all.

In our congregation, we celebrate Gratitude Sunday right before Thanksgiving. Three persons or families tell a story of how they have come to live with gratitude, often growing out of some situation that has caused pain and suffering in their lives. In the recent past, that has included a teenager dealing with being adopted from another country as a baby, a family recovering from their son's drug addition, and a man's loss of employment. Each of the speakers described how difficult that experience was and yet all of them spoke of their gratitude in coming through. Hearing these stories of challenges that have been transformed in some way and joining the teller in giving thanks touches everyone.

On one of the Open and Affirming (O & A) Sundays in our congregation, two couples and one man told stories of how they had overcome the prejudice or bias toward them due to their sexual orientation. On another, a lesbian couple spoke about their commitment service in the congregation, a gay man told how he finally found a Christian church that affirmed both his Christianity and his homosexuality, and a lesbian couple told their story of adopting children. The power of all of the stories shared at those annual Sundays has brought the congregation closer. Welcoming these people and their transforming stories tells of the hospitality that flows out into the whole community.

These stories of the worship services and the ways in which hospitality can be expanded from them leads us to consider the differences between a congregation and the bread company. The community of faith is shaped by the Christian story, the story of the love of God made manifest in the person of Jesus Christ. Jesus's life, death, and resurrection are the heart of the Christian story and shape all that the church is to be and do. This story encompasses the joys and the sufferings of human life, and it invites everyone to practice love and to live with hope since God has first loved us and gives us hope in God's eternal presence. This is a foundational faith affirmation that does distinguish a congregation from a business.

The separation between ourselves and God, and ourselves and others, and even the separation of our ego from our true self, is not overcome in customer service in a bread company! The pain of loneliness might not be met in customer service, of course, while it can be alleviated in a genuine community of faith. The purpose of the church is to be the body of Christ, the place of welcome, the true hospitality of all that we are. Where hospitality is grounded in a vital spiritual life, in the congregation the welcome to long-time members as well as visitors can bring light and healing. What is broken can be mended. Those who are lost can be found. Surely, this happens in congregations where acknowledgment, listening, paying attention, bringing zest, and following up are present.

The framework in which hospitality is embodied in the congregation is typically more expansive, deeper, and more intentionally inclusive than in business. While the ingredients learned from business can be adapted and incorporated into our congregations, congregations can also take them and, in the context of the Christian story, enrich the community life of the congregation over time. For instance, listening to each other and learning about a person's passion for helping others, over time may lead to that person's involvement in a particular mission, a project about a need in the community or the world. In our congregation, at the time of writing this, there have been seven adult mission trips to New Orleans to rebuild homes and lives after Katrina. Because of the Christian story of self-abandoning love that is preached over time, the hospitality toward those who are still seeking to reestablish their home is enacted.[11] In doing so, the reciprocal hospitality from those whose homes we are rebuilding is a confirmation of God's own Spirit alive. So, if the qualities of customer service can be present in businesses whose "bottom line" is the top priority, how much more do they need to be present in congregations whose priority is living out the reign of God? Practicing acknowledgment, listening, paying attention, bringing zest, and following up in the congregation's life may lead to the depth of hospitality that is unique to a congregation.

Business is not church, naturally. However, while we have been looking at the uniqueness of hospitality in a congregation's life from the perspective of customer service in business, we can also look at what insights a congregation may offer to business. There are five insights that I offer to small face-to-face businesses that might give guidance. It does not matter what faith tradition is involved. Each insight from a congregation can also be valuable in a business setting. Several of the chapters in part 1 of this book lift up these insights for businesses.

1. Spirituality points to the dimension of our experience that is beyond what we can immediately see. Living the spirituality learned in a congregation can help businesses extend their welcome. For the depth of our hospitality is a measure of the depth of our spirituality, as I have said. The quality of spirituality can permeate any relationships, including business relationships of customer service. Spirituality is crucial in the hospitality that is authentic.

2. Central to good customer service relationships are encounters that do matter, that do connect. The interaction in business is more than the exchange of goods or services. It is textured by a relationship between two people with real passions and interests, questions and issues. Congregations can shape the ways that members can connect with others by faith. As a result, these members may make a difference in the encounters they have whether or not they are engaged in customer service.

3. The congregation is a communal extension of such connections, and thereby hospitality is alive, it can bring life, just as it can in business. It reminds us that no one can or need go it alone, for life is lived together. The congregation is a "container of hope," as one person put it. It is a place for love and healing. Even though ostensibly businesses do not offer that, they are likewise made up of groups of people who can give support, encouragement, engagement, and who do offer life.

4. Training that is offered by businesses needs to take in account some of the disciplines of spirituality that have been demonstrated in congregations. Practicing spirituality shapes charac-

ter and forms habits of seeing and living in the world. Offering these disciplines to businesses does shape business practices.

5. The congregation's message is that persons are valued just as they are. Hearing the stories of faith, welcome, and inclusion that are positive affirms the grace that is readily available to everyone. Knowing that grace is generously extended to oneself, a person can then be more present with others. As a valued person, the staff person in customer service can welcome and be attentive to the needs of the customer without needing his or her approval. The stories of heart-warming hospitality, even in situations that are uncomfortable, can provide constancy of welcome.

Congregations and customer service staff in businesses can learn much from each other about hospitality even though each one embodies that hospitality both similarly and uniquely. Engendering an atmosphere for telling stories makes spirituality tangible, the encounter significant, the hospitality alive, the training applicable, and the connections sustained.

4

LEARNING FROM CUSTOMER SERVICE IN OTHER BUSINESSES

> *My chance encounter had affirmed a golden*
> *rule in journalism: everyone has a story, so get*
> *out of the office and talk to people. There's no*
> *telling what you might find.*
>
> **—STEVE LOPEZ**[1]

THANKS TO MY TIME AT THE GREAT HARVEST BREAD COMPANY, WHEREVER I go I am now much more aware of how customer service staff treat people. What is it like to be a customer? The following stories of customer service in business will undoubtedly also help you see what is happening in your congregation.

NEGATIVE EXPERIENCES

First, let's look at less satisfying experiences and how they can affect a customer's response to a business interaction. It's not too hard to apply the parallels to our congregations.

Robotic Responses

It feels to me as if the customer service staff in my local grocery store is a little cloying. They always begin with, "Did you find everything you wanted?" After I use my credit card at the check out, they give me the receipt and say, "Thank you, Mr. Johnson," and ask if I need help carrying my two small bags to the car. I know they are trying. I know that they have had some kind of training. But their responses seem robotic. Modifying their responses to make them more spontaneous would make the situation feel more human. Remembering a checkout conversation about traveling in Italy convinces me that it's possible. Self-checkout lines may be efficient, but without any human interaction, all hope for connection and hospitality is lost.

In her book *Untamed Hospitality*, Elizabeth Newman describes the wonderful movie *Babette's Feast*. In the movie, Babette finds refuge with an austere group of Danish puritans. After fourteen years, Babette, who is in fact a renowned Parisian chef, comes into some money and surprises her hosts by preparing a lavish feast. The puritans soften a bit and their warmth begins to shine through. Newman writes, "Grace-filled hospitality takes time. . . . Whereas the global market aims for efficiency and speed, Christian hospitality is content to wait, to take time, to apparently do nothing if need be, since the aim is to be in God's abundant time of giving and receiving rather than in efficient, productive time."[2] In robotic time, even the waiting is not filled with blessing and richness. It is steely, unimaginative, and empty.

I was getting to know many return customers at the bread company as the months continued. There were ways to build on the prior encounters as long as I could remember the customer's name or something about which we had talked. I made this effort partly because of the negative, robotic encounters I experienced at my local video store despite interacting with the same cashier there week after week.

No Relationships

After doing the paperwork to enter a ski race at a lodge one winter, I asked the desk clerk about the activities for that evening. He did not have a clue. I scrabbled around and found information right there on the counter in a newsletter that had been printed off by the staff. The clerk looked around and then indicated that the time of the evening's activities had been misprinted. He did not inform me where the activities were to be held, nor did he check to make sure I knew how to get there. He did not reach out to me at all, although his being the guests' chief point of connection at the lodge's welcome and information counter would lead one to expect that to be his role.

I notice the same misstep with sales people in stores as they hand me my receipt. One day the salesperson did not get off the phone, just nodded to me as she gave me my receipt and kept right on talking. She hardly acknowledged me as a person, although I was right in front of her!

I used to go into the bank to make my deposits and withdraw cash with my bank card. Now the bank has moved and there are three drive-up areas so that there is no need to talk with anyone face to face. At the ATM machine drive-through, there is not even a disembodied voice. I have talked with customer service personnel in the bank before. There had been some interaction. Now there is none. Sit in the car, do your banking, and leave without a word. One more time efficiency has replaced a human encounter.

Can't there at least be recognition of the human being who is in front of you, even at the checkout? I recall the sobering story by Albert Camus about the teacher who came into the classroom looking for a student after the class had ended. Looking around, the teacher's eyes stopped for a couple seconds on the one student who was in the classroom. Recognizing that this student was not the one he was looking for, the teacher left without a word. The student became an object, a thing in the teacher's eyes. A brief interaction would not have been so difficult.

Negative Vibes

In one store, I asked the server, "How are you?" wanting to acknowledge him and see what kind of response he might offer. "Okay," he responded. "Particularly if the store can stay open and I can get my bonus!" he continued. Really, I thought. Would I want to continue coming to this store to shop? Would I be doing so in order to help keep it going and help my server receive his bonus? On the other hand, I wondered, will I feel guilty if I do not go back? Or will I decide not to go back because the exchange was not very enjoyable?

At a supermarket, the cashier seemed grumpy. She did not look at me as I was putting items on the conveyor belt, did not even make the customary inquiries about finding everything. So I asked her, "How are you doing today?" "Not well," she said. That was that. "I am sorry," I said. "I do hope it gets better." No response. Just bagging the groceries. It felt as if I were invisible and my comments were unheard. I thought, "She is engaged in some inner battle and is making it felt to those around her."

Even brief verbal exchanges can carry a positive or negative tone. Meyer writes, "I cringe when a waiter asks, 'How is everything?' That's an empty question that will get an empty response. I abhor the question, 'Are you still working on the lamb?' If the guest has been *working on* the lamb, it probably wasn't very tender or very good in the first place."[3] I also concur with Meyer that when the guest says "thank you," and the waiter or the salesperson at the store says in response, "No problem," there is in fact a problem! For, "Since when is it necessary to deny that delivering excellent service is a 'problem'? A genuine 'You're welcome' is always the appropriate response."[4]

Once at the checkout counter in a large discount store, I mentioned to the checkout person that I worked at the counter of the Great Harvest Bread Company. "So you know what it is like!" she said with an exasperated tone. Even a small comment like that carries weight. Was she burned out by the hectic pace of the work? Does she like the work, or is she harried by the constant stream of customers? I assume many customers ask similar questions or seem demanding. Is that depleting for the staff? Yes, of course this kind of work is depleting. She was not able to carry on a conversation, just heaved a sigh of exasperation.

The repetitive and fast-paced activities in a congregation likewise make it a challenge to settle down and offer a centered, gracious welcome. Often before a service begins in a congregation, those who come at the last minute rev up the frenzy in the welcoming area. It can leave the welcomers frazzled and discouraged that a potential connection could not be made. One way to deal with this is for the welcomer to take a breath and remember that the way the connection is being made is by that first encounter. Be calm in the eye of the storm.

Before turning to the positives, we might surmise some of the reasons why there are negative experiences and why we experience negative vibes. As a couple of the examples indicate, there are people in customer service who are not happy: not happy with their salary, perhaps not happy about their hours, perhaps not happy with their coworkers, perhaps exhausted from being on their feet all day, or perhaps frazzled by having a very short break time. The way that the employees are treated will inevitably rub off on the way that the customers are treated. To feel invisible and be unacknowledged as staff will thwart a connection and usually sink the practice of positive hospitality. If businesses were to implement some of the insights that I have learned from my time at the counter as well as modify those qualities of hospitality from a congregation, I believe there would be fewer negative experiences and it could reduce the negative vibes.

POSITIVE EXPERIENCES

I can also tell many stories that show positive customer service, even in the very same stores in which more negative ones happened. This makes me wonder whether there is a different training for some staff or if the staff people are themselves different.

Relationships

Once a cashier asked about the Children's Hospital at which I worked since my credit card indicated no tax for business. She mentioned a friend whose child had been there and had recovered. "It must be so hard to be there with the sick children," she said. It was a real comment, a real engagement, even though it was very brief. Her human comment allowed another world of experience to enter the conversation.

Another cashier, this time at a large discount store, asked about my work at the Children's Hospital. He seemed somewhat familiar to me but I did not remember him. "How did you know?" I asked. "I remember the bracelets you are wearing," he said. He had remembered that from several months before. I was impressed.

As I was checking out a movie at the video store, a cashier said, "That's a good movie. Have you seen this one, too?" gesturing to another one. We talked for a while. This is the same store where a different staff member had been robotic in her response. This cashier was engaging and upbeat, which brings back to mind the adage, "Hire the right staff and hospitality happens."

In a bank where I was a customer, the customer service person likewise asked me about my bracelets. "Are they for raising money?" she asked. "I wear each of them because they remind me of a person or situation," I responded. Noticing the green one, she asked, "Have you given an organ?" "No, but the son of one of our congregation's members received a heart transplant. I wear it for him and his family. Also I think about the person whose death allowed my friend's son to receive a heart." "Well," she replied, "I must admit I don't think much about those difficult things. I haven't had to experience such hard things yet." It was an authentic conversation and made the business transaction enjoyable and connecting.

Positive Vibes

When I leave my local discount warehouse after shopping, as is the custom I give the receipt to the person at the door to check that I've not been charged twice for something (or am not leaving with something not paid for). Almost all the time, the person makes eye contact before taking the sales receipt to check it. The exchange is brief, about five seconds. But one day as a man returned my receipt, rather than the typical "Have a good day" response I'd expected, he said with honest feeling, "Have a wonderful evening." The genuineness of his response took me aback. At my next visit, the same staff person took my receipt, checked it, and said "goodnight" without even looking at me. The simple and brief encounter is not always welcoming. But with a little effort, it can be.

Yet at the same store, when a two- to three-year-old boy sitting in his mother's cart handed the receipt to the staff person, she drew a face of a pilot on the receipt and handed it back to the boy. His face lit up and he squealed with joy. It was an original and amusing way to connect.

At the warehouse, the encounter is very brief as I roll my shopping cart out of the store. What can transpire in that amount of time? Will *I* thank them, have eye contact with them, smile or nod at them? Will *they* thank me, have eye contact with me, smile at me, or nod to me before I leave? These small transactions can make a good experience. I believe, however, that it is up to the customer service staff to take the first step.

SUMMARY

Spirituality means at least "paying attention" in the interpersonal connections we have. So notice how you are being treated when you are in the grocery store line, at the department store, or in the hardware store. What does it tell you about how the staff has been trained? What do you surmise about the intention of the staff in what they are doing? What comes across about the staff's personality?

When I was a customer at two of the restaurants in New York City that were opened by Danny Meyer, I paid particular attention to the ways that the staff dealt with us. The staff were personal without being overbearing, gracious without being ingratiating, and they picked up on the signals of what we wanted almost before we mentioned anything. I have also witnessed the incredible hospitality of a woman in a very large congregation who welcomed almost everyone by name, and who recognized who was visiting. I have seen a person who was a newcomer to a congregation become within four months a key welcomer at the services. "Emulating someone is a good way to learn hospitality. Find a hospitable person and spend time with them. Listen to them. Do not look for methods or tips from them. Just be together and you will be astonished at what happens."[5]

I watch my colleagues at the bread company interact with the customers. They are upbeat, smiling as they offer bread. My empathy grows as I see them interact with customers. One comment can be important; one glance at the customer makes a difference. My colleagues make me more conscious of my own role and the way I interact with others.

Those same skills of discernment about hospitality and connection apply in your own congregation. After all, you can see what is happening. You can feel what it is like. You can think about what you know. So now apply your reflective experiences in the business world to your engagement in your congregation. Is there dissonance? Is there harmony? If the same intention is to make someone else feel like a genuine human being in both worlds, doesn't it make sense to develop those qualities in both worlds?

5

TRAINING PEOPLE FOR YOUR SETTING

*Trust lies at the heart of a functioning, cohesive
team. Without it, teamwork is all but impossible.
Unfortunately, the word* trust *is used—and
misused—so often that it has lost some of its
impact and begins to sound like motherhood and
apple pie . . . trust is the confidence among team
members that their peers' intentions are good,
and that there is no reason to be protective or
careful around the group. In essence, teammates
must get comfortable being vulnerable with
one another.*

PATRICK LENCIONI[1]

WHETHER IN A BUSINESS OR A CONGREGATION, IT IS THE PEOPLE WHO
make it a hospitable place to be and therefore who need encouragement and training. Yet as we shall see it is also the setting of the congregation that makes a difference.

STAFF TRAINING

My on-the-job training at the Great Harvest Bread Company began with some "apron time" during the second portion of my job interview. That meant spending an hour or two at the front counter, dealing with the customers and the baked goods being sold. It was energizing. It was comfortable. It was also a tad unnerving since I had absolutely no direction for those first hours. Perhaps that was the goal. "Let's see how a new person might jump into the water and swim without any instruction. Will they have the resourcefulness, fluidity, and chutzpah to make it a go?" The staff was all the more willing to give guidance since, I assumed, they had also learned on the job. I had absolutely no "let's sit down and go over the procedures and functions of your job" orientation. It was learn as you go, ask as you need, and receive directions as given. It made the job energizing.

At first, my priority at the bread company was to provide the customer with delicious and nutritious bread. What came to me next was to see how the staff would interact with each other in order to make sure that first priority was met. It was the staff who did most of the training and who provided the guidance for how to meet my priority of serving the customer. When I experienced the dynamism of the staff and how we could work together as a team, I felt the connective tissue that made us cohesive. When the staff worked together, the customer was served well.

Unfortunately, there wasn't much time to interact with each other as staff members, so I had to pay attention in the brief encounters I had with them. Staff stories could be told or listened to, although when the customers entered the store the conversations ended. I learned of Lisa's blended family because we walked together to the bank so I could learn how to get the change we needed. I had a few minutes as we were bagging the rolls to hear about Mary's visit to a college in California where she was seeking admission. Several weeks later as we stood at the bread board together I learned she had been admitted. As Chad and I walked down the aisle between the sandwiches and the slicing machine, I learned of his quandary about his mother-in-law's demands. While slicing bread I celebrated with

Jennifer in her training for a half marathon. James' bandaged arm indicated his skateboarding injury, and at the sandwich board I learned of David's desire to learn more about computers. While we were to be focused on the customer, it was not only congenial to get to know each other a little, but enjoying each other in turn spilled over to our encounters with our customers.

Much of our interstaff conversations were like sound bites. Brief and to the point. Especially when we would kid each other, or say something humorous, the customer could pick up the light energy in the exchange. For instance, when the local newspaper had an article about Mary's "slack rope" competition, we posted it, celebrated her accomplishments, and kidded her about her balance. There may have been more staff interaction than I was aware of since I was only there part time. In fact, many staff did go together on a weekend raft trip organized and paid by the store owner. However, we exchanged relatively few sentences with each other during our working time since our energy was spent on the customers. Of course, we covered each other for breaks and each of us could jump in and do what was needed to make the business hum. We shared our individual gifts, just as the body of many parts work together for the whole. Everyone is important and each has a part and some are interchangeable. This image of a community of many parts working together is familiar to those who know St. Paul's description of the "body" of the congregation.[2]

In light of this section about the staff's interactions and staff training, the priority that Meyer puts on the staff of his restaurant is laudable. It only became clear to me after several months at the bread company what a crucial role staff have through their interactions with the customers. At first, I thought it was the customer who was the primary focus of our work. While customers are highly significant, of course, the role of the staff grew in importance the longer I worked at the bread company. Alongside this insight, I recalled my first experience while being a chaplain in the hospital. It is natural to think that the patients in the hospital are the highest priority in the chaplain's work. That was my total focus, I thought at first. Then it became clear to me that the hospital staff, the whole team that worked with patients, was just as important. The staff working together makes the patient more comfortable, creates an environment that is more conducive to healing, and together offers patient-centered care.

Adapting this to the congregational setting, when the church staff is working together in sync in response to the church's mission, the members are energized in their own ministries, they are energized by the staff's energy, and they are confident in the overall church's mission. This does not take away from the importance of the customer, the patient, or the church member. It is just that in the context of practicing hospitality, the staff is crucial. The concept of "enlightened hospitality" is what Meyer calls the five components of how a restaurant functions smoothly.

What comes first are the employees, the staff. Without the business nurturing, training, and supporting them, the whole operation comes apart. We have noted that one of the reasons that there may be negative vibes in a business is because the staff is not appreciated. When the staff complain about the working conditions, their salaries, or how hard they are asked to work, the conditions are set up for such negativity. That is not good for the customer, let alone for the physical and perhaps spiritual condition of each staff person. I recall one experience at the local grocery store when the cashier did not respond to my greeting. She grunted as she picked up the items to scan. I said, "Bad day?" I was in my groove of checking on how customers were being treated. Then she said that she had just come back from a doctor's appointment and was sick. I empathized and said I hoped that she would feel better soon. If a manager had known about her condition, perhaps she would have been given a break or asked to do something else until she felt better, or, if she was badly ill, the manager could have relieved her. Even if her financial position obliged her to stay at work, the manager might at least have offered sympathy and shown some compassion and thanked her for continuing to work. Meyer writes, "it is the value of the human experience we have with our colleagues (staff)—what we learn from one another, how much fun we have working together, and how much mutual respect and trust we share—that has the greatest influence on job satisfaction."[3] At the bread company, the staff is encouraged to make their own sandwiches for lunch as well as to select a loaf of bread to take home every day they work. This is a way to appreciate the staff. On Halloween, there is a costume contest among the staff, the owner chooses the best costume for the day, and there is a reward. The staff has fun. So, the staff is first on the list of Meyer's "enlightened hospitality."

Second are the guests. They are the ones who will benefit from the staff's customer service and the dishes that are created by the cooking staff. The example of the cashier in the illustration above shows the way that the customer will benefit from or be put off by the staff. At the bread store the owner was always alert to how quickly the customers were being served or how long they were waiting. If the staff were talking among themselves while the customer was waiting to be served, the owner usually had a few sharp words to say to us!

Maya Angelou tells a story of when she and a friend were at a restaurant in the south many years ago. They were the only African Americans in the place. After placing their order, they waited for more than thirty minutes and still had not been served. Maya decided that it was because of their skin color, so she called the waitress over to say that if they were not going to be served they would leave. The waitress in her southern drawl indicated that the chef had run out of grits, but now that he had gotten more, they would very soon be serving everyone. She pointed out that in fact all the customers were waiting since the restaurant did not serve a breakfast without grits. Maya mumbled an apology and grimaced at her own embarrassment. What I like about this story is that the waitress was doing the best she could. Yet she could have anticipated the customers' frustration and mentioned the reason for the long wait before Maya became annoyed. Meyer writes that, in his restaurants, "guests know when a host is insincere, harried, or just going through the motions in greeting and seating them. It's not genuine hospitality when the host fails to make eye contact, fails to smile, or fails to thank the guests for coming."[4] The focus here is on the customer, and by extension the focus in a congregation should be on a visitor.

The third component for a smooth-running restaurant is the community. This was a new concept for me. The interaction with the community in which the restaurant resides is very important. The Union Square Café in New York City, started by Meyer, became very involved in the reclamation of Union Square, the neighborhood near the café. Many restaurants joined together to raise funds for a plethora of causes over the years. One of the goals was to get the restaurants out of their four walls—a good insight for congregations as well. Meeting the people in the neighborhood, discerning the needs that were present locally, providing food for community events and for a local hospice, joining the causes that also touched the staff members, and being a good citizen in the wider community were just a part of what it meant to be engaged with the community. In response to the September 11, 2001, attack on the Twin Towers and in the aftermath of the Katrina hurricane in 2005, Meyer and his staff responded with support, encouragement, and sustenance. Especially regarding September 11, 2001, after which he had doubts about whether restaurants were important, he writes, "I answered my own doubts. In their ability to nourish and nurture, and to provide a buoyant place for human beings to be with one another, and to smile, restaurants—as a healing agent—seemed more relevant than ever."[5] Contrary to the Simon and Garfunkel song, businesses and congregations are not islands. They feel pain and sometimes even cry at the human need around. The response is not to shrink down and withdraw, but rather to reach out and engage. This energy brings vitality. It makes a difference by not being enclosed but rather engaging with the surrounding physical environment.

The fourth component for a smooth-running restaurant is suppliers. They are the ones who bring the goods to the restaurant. The perspective that Meyer offers in deciding who will bring the supplies for his restaurants is this. "Of course pricing is an important calculation; but for us, excellence, hospitality, and shared values must also be prominent factors in the selection process."[6] Even dealing with the suppliers means that there are relationships that are developed, and the strategies for deciding what to select are based on a value laden perspective. In order to engage with the suppliers, it is important to be clear about the way the business is living in the world and what mission or purpose they are trying to live out. It then is incumbent on the suppliers, as well, to delineate their purposes and values. While this may seem too unbusinesslike, it actually is a foundation for being in business, at least in a business that is worthy, productive, and increases the well-being of people and the environment.

The fifth component is investors. Who is going to support the effort of developing a new project or to underwrite an ongoing program? In order for that to happen, the one who is proposing the project or running the program will have to put his or her own personal resources on the line. Meyer puts it this way, "It gives comfort and confidence to an outside investor . . . to know that those of us charged with running the business have our own 'skin' in the game."[7] Self-investment is the first step to getting investors to invest! If a project is going to grow, it usually means there needs to be others who will join in the development and implementation of the project. Otherwise, flying solo, while fun, will not expand the program.

As I mentioned in the introduction, I have learned how to make biscotti. I call them the "Beloved Biscotti" because Henri Nouwen used the word "beloved" in such a powerful way and I got the recipe from a person who was entertaining the director of the Henri Nouwen Foundation years ago. Now I make them for one local café. When I was asked to consider expanding my small kitchen business to sell the biscotti to up to a hundred cafés, I demurred. Do I want to use my energy in this way? Is this a life mission? I know that I could hire other people to help me do this. I know that I could find some investors to launch this business. However, at the time of this writing, it is not the right thing to do. Meyer told his investors that he put his own funds as well as his "skin" into his vision but that the profitability of the project would be slow and gradual. He writes, "I was far more focused on excellence and hospitality than on profitability. Today, earning a profit is still not the primary destination for my business, but I know that it is the fuel that drives everything else we do."[8] Eventually the investors will benefit from all the aforementioned components if all of them are working well. A whole chapter of Meyer's book is dedicated to this concept and to the way enlightened hospitality works.[9] I can still find joy in supplying one café with my Beloved Biscotti, and since the goal is not to be profitable in this arena, I have more energy to put my "skin" into other projects in which there are many more "investors" who share my convictions and values.

Enlightened hospitality can apply to our congregations as we focus our energies on our ministry of hospitality. In training welcomers and ushers, we are creating that climate in which the welcome of visitors and one another is a sign of our faithful commitment to the message of hospitality. However, this training is put in the wider and deeper context of inclusion that is at the heart of God's welcome of us. St. Paul writes in Romans 15:7, "Welcome one another, therefore, just as Christ has welcomed you, for the glory of God." If it were merely because a person is gregarious and outgoing that he or she welcomes others, that behavior would probably not persist over time. Personal gregariousness might also not be enough for someone to welcome those who are different than himself or herself. Welcome is reaching out with a gracious invitation to those who are not engaged in a faith community. This includes the stranger and the person who feels like an outsider. That is where the Spirit is present and is working. In order to be able to do this, just as in a business, a church does well to spend energy on training, encouragement, and resources for those who are the welcomers in the congregation.

It is difficult, I believe, to find the time and the energy to offer training for welcomers. Just having people who are willing to do this every Sunday often seems to be effort enough. However, even a little training can make a huge difference. Giving volunteers some background about the power of welcoming, connecting with others, and the human need for such human contact and support is a good place to begin. There may be three training session beyond the initial conversation about what the role of the welcomer may be. These sessions ought to grow out of the work of a membership committee, for instance, whose mission and purpose is clear from the beginning. After outlining some ideas for training sessions, I will give an example from one church's mission statement regarding membership.

What might such training sessions look like? First, after introductions, pose the question: "Where have you experienced welcome in a business? In a congregation?" After reflecting as a group, list the ingredients that have come to the surface in those experiences. Then ask a second question: "Where did you not feel welcome? What was that like?" Then once again reflect on the ingredients that made for the negative experience of hospitality. As a group, come up with some statements of affirmation about how hospitality does and can work in your congregation. Also include statements of what you do not want to happen in your ministry of hospitality. Between this first meeting and the second, invite each person to notice how he or she experiences hospitality in businesses and in church.

At the second session, share your experiences since the first meeting. Then, explore some of the biblical stories about hospitality, in particular, the story of Zacchaeus. What does it feel like to be Zacchaeus? What do you think transformed him? Meditate on St. Paul's words to the church in Rome to "[w]elcome one another as Christ has welcomed you." Share stories and/or your experiences about being welcomed by Christ's love. Ask each person to notice one situation between the second and the third session when hospitality would have been appropriate and how one might have responded.

At the third session, share stories of what has been happening during the interim. Then begin to reflect on ways in which hospitality can grow and develop in your congregation. This is a time to share the mission statement by one church that took on the challenge to develop a ministry of hospitality and develop a mission statement for this team. Follow the mission statement with writing some specific strategies to implement that mission. (See the paragraphs following the next one for the sample mission statement and several suggested strategies to accomplish it.).

The ongoing structure of the hospitality team will be to have a membership committee or whatever your church would call it. In our congregation, we continue meeting monthly to reflect on our experience, sign on for the upcoming responsibilities, raise new ideas for enriching the hospitality, and support each other. As I learned over the years, a good meeting has the "four-legged stool" foundation. First is experiencing the team as a community. That means "checking in" to see what has been happening recently in a person's life. Second, have an agenda so that the meeting will have structure and form. Third, include action steps, not just conversation. And fourth, provide some spiritual support. That may happen by opening with a reading and a prayer as well as closing the meeting with prayer. Making sure that these ingredients are included in a meeting will provide a meaningful time for the team. It will also be an arena in which ongoing training happens. The slogan is true that for many people it is easier to act their way into a new way of thinking than thinking their way into a new way of acting. In action oriented training, the hospitality team will learn, grow, and be enriched.

Here is one church's membership committee statement, referred to previously, which you can share with your team as an example: "The mission of this committee is to infuse the qualities and experiences of invitation, hospitality, and incorporation throughout the church community." Its strategies are:

1. Teaching and developing programs about being a growing church

2. Helping people find the words and the attitude of reaching out to others with a warm invitation to the church and the life of the church

3. Evaluating the church's hospitality from the time a person comes to the church until he or she leaves the church

4. Developing appropriate approaches to welcome visitors as well as long time members

5. Assisting the ministers with new members' classes

6. Keeping up with the new members to assist in ways to incorporate them into the active life of the church

As we have a fairly large church, we have nine members on this committee, each with a three-year commitment. Each year three members rotate off the committee and we elect three new members.

THE SETTING

The Great Harvest Bread Company store is actually one very large room. When customers come in, they see almost everything that is going on, except for seeing the wheat that is being ground by stone in a small room in the back of the store. The bakers, sandwich makers, and servers are all visible. That makes for a lot of movement and varied activities. Customers come into an ongoing, vital, and busy environment. One cannot help but be energized by the energy! On top of that, especially in the mornings when the baking is happening, customers step into the store, inhaling the yeasty smells of baking bread with an expectation of delight. They are glad to be at the store. Along with the intoxicating smells, a variety of musical offerings from more than thirty radio stations creates an ambience of upbeat appreciation.

REFLECTION AND APPLICATIONS

The environment in which our religious activities happen can likewise either inhibit or augment the spiritual encounters that are at the heart of our activities. Because our environment affects our experience, we do well to pay attention to how the place looks. What is it telling us? Is it crowded and cramped or airy and open? How does it smell? Are there signs of energy and activity in the surroundings as well as in the people? Is it well lit or dim and dingy? Is it clean or messy? Can people hear well? Is the music pleasing, welcoming, and engaging?

At the bread store all of the senses are engaged. Is that the case in your congregation? There are many people in our congregation who are sensates—meaning that their senses are tuned to what the environment is saying. When I visit a church I look at the colors, the cleanliness, the way the seating is arranged, and how the front of the church is laid out. Those say a lot about the church. My experience at the bread company is that the environment is very welcoming.

Look at what the environment in your congregation is saying about how welcoming it is.

The welcomers are actually part of the environment. What are they conveying? What does their presence say to the visitors? How are they interacting with the newcomers as well as the long-time members? There are special gifts that are helpful for those who are on the front line at a service in the congregation. Who in the congregation discerns what gifts congregation members have for engaging in the ministry of hospitality? In many congregations there may be an "Inventory of Talents and Time" where a person self-identifies their "special gifts" as a greeter or welcomer; however, it usually helps to have a person or two in the congregation who understand the skills needed for the ministry of hospitality and invite particular people for this ministry. When recruiting these volunteers, does the invitation include discerning those who are joyful, whose attitudes are open, and whose hearts are welcoming? Are the greeters, welcomers, and ushers upbeat, pleasant people? They are the first people anyone will encounter as they arrive. When these people respond to the invitation positively, be sure to have a qualified person offer the training and the guidance for enhancing the spirit of welcome through these people.

The staff and the environment are key ingredients in shaping the experience of hospitality in a business as well as in a congregation. Using Meyer's enlightened hospitality, consider how your congregation might look at your emphasis on staff, or members (guests), or community, or administration (suppliers), or active contributors (investors.) Seeing your ministry of hospitality through the lens of business practices of hospitality may guide your congregation to enhance your welcome.

6

CREATING CONTINUITY THROUGH STORIES OF HOSPITALITY

> *Story re-orders, sifts through experience, and allows others, young children and adults alike, to hear what we think truly matters. We are constituted by the stories we tell ourselves and others. Thus stories serve an ontological purpose. Story connects us with that which lies beyond ourselves and this process makes us ask questions about the meanings of our lives.*

—BARBARA KLIMES MYERS[1]

A PERSON'S RELATIONSHIP TO GOD AND TO A COMMUNITY OF FAITH develops over time just as a relationship develops in contexts where hospitality is offered. That can be in a congregation and in a bread store, as had happened for me. A relationship grows when a person pays attention to the details, remembers the story line, and engages in conversation repeatedly. Continuity through several encounters is possible and it strengthens the relationship. In the telling and in the hearing of the stories, the community at the bread company is built up. The following stories illustrate what also may and does happen in our congregations. However, it does mean being attentive to the encounter in which hospitality can be offered. From these encounters the community deepens and is enriched.

JASON

Jason is a university film student who, I learn, is making a film for his course. Each time he comes into the bread store, he is excited about shooting his film. He tells me he has a great cast and crew. The script he has been working on for a long time is coming together. I learn the plot line over the course of several of Jason's lunchtime visits.

Jason comes in scruffy one day. "What's up?" I ask. "Been working on my film project and the insurance for the rental van was held up for four hours," he says. "That pushed me to do more shooting." I ask him to tell me more about his film and he does. He says he'll invite me to the showing when the movie's finished. One day Jason brings his mom into the store to have some bread and introduces her to me. "Where are you from?" I ask. She was from a state close by but now lives in Colorado. "Are you in your son's film?" "No. I support it, though! He has done other ones, too. They are really good." It has taken many visits at the bread counter for me to connect and learn as much as I have about the energy Jason has put into his current film and his financial costs. It also means I have been interested and have pursued the encounter with questions.

One day Jason comes in all shaven. "So, the film is done?" I ask. "Yes, it's in the production studio where they will be making the DVDs," he tells me.

Days later he comes in for a sandwich and I learn that he is still working on the film. "The special effects person stopped working on the project. I have called someone else to do it. I want it to be the best that I can so I am waiting on the call back." I have learned so many details of his movie-making process over the four months that I have known him. The project goes up and down. There are details, unmet expectations, and still he has the energy to continue. Listening to Jason reminds me of the passionate commitment needed to follow through on a vision and to bring life to that vision. The project continues and I hope our relationship also continues. However, since he is a student, realistically that might be the extent of our connection. Even so, I've enjoyed it.

TOM

Tom had been a student at the local university but is now on a new path. Over many visits to the store, I learn he was pre-med in microbiology but did not like it. He tells me that he was not doing what he really wanted to do. As Tom comes in regularly, I have become more and more acquainted with his story. He's applying to graduate school. He shares that many years ago he was diagnosed with a bipolar brain disorder and schizophrenia. "I have had shock therapy and had been on up to forty pills a day. Now I am down to three a day. I have been clean for two years, no illegal drugs and alcohol." That day we shake hands twice. I have worked in organizations that addressed these issues and therefore I have a particular empathy for Tom.

Tom comes in one day and is brimming with new news. He has been admitted to the school of his choice and has received a partial scholarship. I celebrate by giving him a free oatmeal chocolate cookie! He is on his new path.

BILLY

A student comes in and I notice his book on Rene Descartes. "I think, therefore I am," Billy quotes Descartes. "Today, in class it became clear to me. To say 'I don't think that I am' is in itself a contradiction since if I am thinking at all, I am." He talks about his search for wisdom. "To learn about so many people who have ideas about wisdom and even theories of epistemology makes it confusing," he says. I paraphrase words of William James—that it is easier to act your way into a new way of thinking than think your way into a new way of acting. "It seems to me that acting leads into the new ways to see the world and the self in the world."

It is a good thought as we lean over the counter together as others are standing around. I have the sense that he really wants to be engaged. He is staying at the counter, even as he looks off into the distance for a while. He is either processing his thought or not sure what to say next. I look right at him all the time, blocking out other activity around me. It is intense and I sense it is needed.

One of the next times Billy comes in looking for a slice of bread, I learn he finished his class just before spring break and handed in his paper on Descartes. Wittgenstein is next. He's hesitant and seems to want to engage in a conversation. "You know during this school break I want to stop thinking about philosophy. And I just can't do it." "Perhaps meditation," I suggest. "How do you do it?" he asked. "You find a mantra; pay attention to your breathing even for one minute or fifteen seconds at the beginning." "I can't even do that," he says. "I can't turn off my thinking." We're quiet while he butters his bread. An idea pops into my head, "What about exercises like running?" His eyes light up. "Great idea," he responds. "Then as you run look around, see what is there, and smile."

The last time I see him I ask how things are going. "I got an A on my paper on Wittgenstein," he says. I give him a thumbs-up sign, the only way to congratulate him since the sandwich lines are long. Yet another brief encounter of affirmation.

A FAMILY

A family comes in regularly. The family includes two boys, Jensen and Colton, about nine and eleven years old, and a daughter, Jaden, who is three. Sometimes the boys and the dad, Craig, come in after school, or at other times wearing cycling clothes. I've shared with the boys many jokes I've taken from the children's magazine *Highlights*. I give the boys several brainteasers during the usually regular Wednesdays when they come for lunch in the summer.

We talk about my going to New Orleans with my congregation's adult work trip. As a result, Craig gives me twenty dollars to put toward our fund-raiser for the New Orleans Habitat for Humanity program. When I return from the trip, I bring in and show him the photo album of more than one hundred photos. We share issues and concerns beyond the bread that has initially brought us together.

When this family comes in, their daughter, Jaden, usually gets a breadstick. At first, I would invite her to take one. Eventually, she finds the courage to ask me for one.

She comes in one day holding out a soft puzzle she has received for her third birthday. As I sit down on a step in order to be at eye level with her, I ask her what kind of birthday cake she has. "Black," she says. Her mom whispers, "Chocolate." When I ask about a song, she recalls that everyone at the party had sung "Happy Birthday" to her. She is confident, clear, and energetic. Trust has developed between us over the course of three months. One day she runs up to me as I am having lunch and gives me a hug. It feels like pure grace.

One day when Craig asks how I am doing, I tell him I have just had a heart scan and that the news is not altogether good. I ask him if he has had a heart scan. "No," he says. "That might be a good idea," I say. His wife, Tracy, overhearing, nods her head in agreement.

The next time they come in, he has the results of his heart scan. We talk about ways to keep the calcium score low and his wife says appreciatively, "Talking with you is like having a second opinion." I have connected with Craig out of my own experience and at least my experience has encouraged one dad to pay attention. Days later he tells me that he has had a conference with his heart doctor, who has put him on a statin for his heart. "That will keep my heart healthy," he says, reassured.

The preceding stories reveal the many facets of the encounters we can enjoy by giving time and attention. It is too strong to say that we can become family through these connections at the bread store, but they do offer a genuine means of breaking down isolation and give a possible setting for strengthening human bonds. I tell these stories about the students and the family to indicate that continuity builds community when one is in tune with the stories of people's lives.

These are the very same ingredients in a congregation where care and attentiveness are offered.

How can we in a congregation affirm that we are a community of faith if the people in the community are not engaged with each other? Of course, there are many people who are committed to listening and speaking to each other in their congregation. Of course, there typically are deeper connections in a congregation than what I have known at the bread counter. However, the customer service staff at the small face-to-face business is an equal opportunity welcomer. Hospitality is the door for community to be formed. And that means being open and receiving everyone—a good practice for our congregations as well as our businesses.

Yet I also know that in many congregations the conversations are brief, even as brief as those at the counter. Before the service or after the service people congregate with the people they know and with whom they feel comfortable. That leaves out many people who do not know much about each other. It is the responsibility of welcomers to mingle and to find ways to connect people when possible. If someone is visiting, it is important to learn just enough to introduce that person to someone else who has been attending for a while. In order to do that, however, the welcomer needs to know the regular attendees and to know enough to connect them with the visitor. Over time, such attentiveness and even inquisitiveness grows community.

PART TWO | PREPARING THE TABLE

7

OFFERING THE BREAD OF LIFE:
Hospitality in Our Congregations

To identify the movements of the Spirit in our lives, I have found it helpful to use four words: "taken," "blessed," "broken," and "given." These words summarize my life as a priest because each day, when I come together around the table with members of my community, I take bread, bless it, break it, and give it. These words also summarize my life as a Christian because, as a Christian, I am called to become bread for the world: bread that is taken, blessed, broken, and given. Most importantly, however, they summarize my life as a human being because in every moment of my life somewhere, somehow the taking, the blessing, the breaking, and the giving are happening.

—HENRI NOUWEN[1]

ONE OF THE RICHEST EXPERIENCES FOR ME IS TO GATHER AROUND A table and share food together. Usually stories are shared there too, a recounting of the day's events and glimpses of what hopes or expectations might come next. In the very act of eating together with the stories told and heard, hospitality is present.

Although it might not be physical hunger that brings many people to the congregation, there is often a real hunger for a spiritual connection. The hospitality of the space, the people who welcome, the sharing in worship, the participation in fellowship, the engagement in educational programs, and the invitation to action all combine to provide occasions in which the connection with spirituality can happen. In a congregation, the table is one of the most significant symbols of the shared faith, where a spiritual connection is offered.

In the sacrament of Holy Communion in the Christian tradition, the bread is taken, it is blessed, it is broken, and it is given. We call this "Eucharist," which means to give thanks. Using Nouwen's four words—taken, blessed, broken, and given—we can see ways to become hospitable members in our congregation.

TAKEN

Nouwen writes, "the first step in the spiritual life is to acknowledge with our whole being that we already have been taken."[2] While the word "taken" does not convey the feeling of being special, he says another word that has more warmth is "chosen." He continues, "When I know that I am chosen, I know that I have been seen as a special person. Someone has noticed me in my uniqueness and has expressed a desire to know me, to come closer to me, to love me."[3] In communion the word "taken" describes the act of picking up the bread for the communion. In our congregations, each of us is unique, having our own stories and histories. People are chosen, taken, to be unique and special human beings who are the beloved ones of God. In our congregations, being taken/chosen by God to be beloved ones frees us by being loved. There could be no greater gift than our pointing to the God who is the one who takes/chooses us. This does not mean that others are rejected, however. Embracing the truth of being chosen by God to be a beloved one leads to a deep gratitude. It can also lead us to acknowledge and call forth the chosenness that is for others.

Although the bread has been made before, each particular loaf has not. The ingredients, the shape of the loaf, the temperature of the bread, the patina on the top—these things indicate singularity. So also for people: each person is particular and each needs to be treated in a particular way, as an individual, even as a beloved child of God. There are fascinating things about each person about which very little will ever be discovered unless someone else is willing to acknowledge the reality of each person's individuality and listen to him or her.

In her book of meditations, *Becoming Bread*, Gunilla Norris writes, "Bread is a profound and ancient symbol for life. To grow grain and to store it guaranteed our ancestors the possibility of survival. . . . Flour and salt, the makings of bread, were frequently brought to our early altars. The sacrifices were made in recognition of the fact that we are fundamentally creatures of need. Their offerings were petitions for substance. We have understood from the beginning how dependent and vulnerable we are. We have known that in order to live we will always have to receive and care for the gifts of life."[4]

For me the bread counter is a symbol of our dependence and vulnerability. We are in need of sustenance. We need to take bread. Hospitality offers the slice of bread, acknowledging the particularity of the person who is there. In our congregations, we need to see the uniqueness of the person who is there, who has chosen to be there. By the way the welcomer treats that person, his or her experience of being a beloved one of God might be enhanced. To all who come, the congregation conveys this sense of their having been chosen. This is a way of being a hospitable congregation.

The phrase "daily bread" reminds us of the story during the exile of the Jews, who were led by Moses through the wilderness for forty years, according to the book of Exodus. When people were frustrated by the lack of food in the barrenness of their journey, they were given only the "manna," or bread, which was provided daily by the elements. Bread would appear each morning, last only one day, and could not be kept longer. It could not be stored up. They would take only the portion they needed. It had to be either eaten or shared. This "daily bread" offered the life-sustaining substance to all those who were wandering. This sign was given to the wanderers in the face of their fear, to show them divine support that was available for their journey. The people of faith had to learn how to trust that there would be a sufficient supply of nourishment for tomorrow when tomorrow came. It was only by relying on the grace of God that the people could survive.

There was a *New Yorker* cartoon of a woman picking up an item from what looked like an open-air vegetable display. The sign over the display said, "Fresh Insights." The bread we cut on the bread board was fresh, just as I hope the insights that might come in the connection through the conversations were also fresh. If I fell into routine gestures with a customer, I missed someone who came perhaps hoping to find not only fresh bread but also a genuine insight. When a visitor comes to a congregation, there ought to be freshness in the space and warmth in the welcomers' personality. This sets the table for the feast to begin. The place and the people are taken, are chosen, as is the bread for blessing.

BLESSED

"To give a blessing is to affirm, to say 'yes' to a person's Belovedness," writes Nouwen. "A blessing touches the original goodness of the other and calls forth his or her Belovedness."[5] This is not a usual approach at the bread counter. However, believing in the intrinsic value and worth of every customer has led to some amazing stories. The welcome carried a blessing. That word might not be the one used, although sometimes it would seem appropriate. Other times the gesture and the tone of voice carried the blessing.

"Give us this day our daily bread," is a phrase that we say every Sunday in our congregation. This phrase is from Jesus' answer to his disciples when they asked him how to pray. He did not talk about prayer. He prayed. Congregants who regularly pray this prayer may find the fullness of those words even from reflecting on the blessings that surround them every day. Knowing that you are blessed will more likely move you to offer blessings to others. In the dynamic of hospitality, there is a receiving and a giving. At the bread company, the flowing of positive energy came to me. Then, acting as a conduit, I passed that on to others. I am blessed to be a blessing. This is also a key to a congregation's hospitality.

Yet the prayer phrase begins with "give us." It means putting ourselves into a vulnerable place where we are to ask. We come with open hands that may reflect or lead to an open heart. Coming to buy bread can offer a lesson of being in the moment, in the day, in the experience. All that we all really know about is today. Eventually the bread will spoil if we do not freeze it or eat it. When the bread is fresh, when the warm slice of bread is right out of the oven, it is amazingly delicious. Trusting that what is needed will be available, we can risk asking to receive. "Give us the blessing that we so need."

Janet was a handicapped member of the L'Arche community where Nouwen was a chaplain. During a prayer service, Janet asked for a blessing. Nouwen, the priest, offered a perfunctory blessing, tracing the sign of a cross on her forehead. She said, "No, that does-n't work. I want a real blessing."[6] Later in the service, Henri did offer a "real" blessing and as a result more and more of the attendees of the service lined up for this blessing. Customers at our bread counter probably detected if our greeting was perfunctory and the interaction blasé. Members of the congregation may also experience the same in-hospitable climate if the welcomers are not paying attention, listen-ing, and engaging in a fitting way. The real blessing is the ability to respond to the expressed need.

In our congregations, there are ample opportunities to receive and to offer blessings. Sunday after Sunday, congregants and visitors attend services since the doors are always opened on those days. The practices or disciplines of preparing for those who are coming are necessary in order for those blessings to be received and offered. It might be having nametags available at least for the welcomer, a but-ton saying "Welcomer," a large sign indicating where a visitor might find information, a baked goodie for a first-time visitor, a well-in-formed and trained welcomer, and a form for the visitor to fill out to receive the congregation's newsletter.

Some congregations have a regular "Exploring Membership" gathering for visitors who might be interested in joining the church. That is a time to meet with the clergy and a couple members of the hospitality team, take a tour of the facility, get to know each other, have visitors' questions answered, and, if appropriate, have something to eat. There are also congregations that have a relaxed time with the minister once a month on a Sunday after worship with those who are visitors. It is a time to ask any questions and get to know the minister in an informal setting. The visitors are then typically invited to consider a more structured time to explore membership in the church.

Remembering to have child care during such times is important. They are all blessings, ways to pay attention and connect.

Although blessings do include these activities, blessings also come from waiting and being. To make bread, you need to wait for the dough to rise. It is not possible to make it happen faster. We have heard that patience is a virtue. Waiting without anxiousness can grow patience. That is a blessing. Some people come into the store anxious to get the special bread of the day only to realize that it is still proofing, not even in the oven yet. This is the time to wait.

A *New Yorker* cartoon showed a stolid woman standing at the garden store counter saying, "I would like some bulbs that I can force." We cannot force the bread to rise. We can have the temperature right, yet the yeast will take the time that it takes. The loaves are set aside for a time. Patience is needed. Patiently waiting for the yeast to proof points to the spiritual disciplines of paying attention, letting go, and trusting. In the waiting is the anticipation of what is to be. We do not and cannot make it all happen ourselves.

As we anticipate that new members will join our congregation, we can take the necessary steps to make sure they are shown hospitality. However, we also need patience for the Spirit to work in their lives so they might take the steps that are best for them. Such growth cannot be forced or cajoled. Instead we wait patiently, and with faith. This is where trust comes in, trust in the God who is at work in the lives of those who will visit and in the life of the congregation. In this time of patient and attentive waiting, blessings come.

BROKEN

After "taken," and "blessed," comes "broken." Not everything works out according to our own plans! What we might hope would be perfect does not always turn out that way. At the bread company we want every loaf of bread to be perfect. Just so. Yet there is always the odd loaf with air pockets that consequently does not make for great sandwiches. As the saying goes, practice makes perfect. That is almost true at the store. Thousands of loaves have been baked. We have had lots of practice.

Some welcomers in the congregation may feel like old pros. They get in the routine so much that their flexibility in responding to new people and new situations may become too lax and they may not be particularly alert. When one has the attitude of a beginner, encounters can be fresh and invigorating. When one doesn't assume the dialogue is already scripted, one can see new revelations. In my congregation, when we learned that we needed more than one person as a welcomer and for each of them to be in different locations in the building at different times during the morning, we changed. We looked at things with the perspective of a newcomer, which reminded us to feel like beginners, not like perfect pros.

Congregations do not need to be perfect; in their own incompleteness, wholeness will come. In our own spiritual journeys, it seems to me that our goal is not for perfection but for wholeness. Everything comes together, the imperfect as well, making up the whole. Many artists throughout the world, from Navaho rug weavers to Japanese brush painters, intentionally leave some kind of imperfection in their work to remind themselves as well as the viewer that neither they nor their work is perfect.

As a customer service staff person, at the beginning I wanted to be perfect. To do everything not only right but better than better was my goal. It was my own inadequacy that fueled the desire to be perfect. When that desire to be perfect is expressed, it sends dissonant vibes to those around. It brings a sense of rigidity and tension. It does not animate and energize. What I needed to learn was to accept my imperfection and find the flow.

In *The Spirituality of Imperfection* we read, "The spirituality of imperfection begins with the recognition that trying to be perfect is the most tragic human mistake . . . the book *Alcoholics Anonymous* suggests, 'First of all, we had to quit playing God.' According to the way of life that flows from this insight, it is only by ceasing to play God, by coming to terms with errors and shortcomings, and by accepting the inability to control every aspect of their lives that any human beings can find the peace and serenity that alcohol (or drugs, sex, money, material possessions, power, or privilege) promise but never deliver."[7]

The recognition of the brokenness in our common humanity may lead to a richness that is unexpected. In order for the bread to be eaten or shared, it has to be broken. Nouwen wrote about the Eucharist in his book *Compassion*. "There are very few places left in our world where our common humanity can be lifted up and celebrated, but each time we come together around the simple signs of bread (and wine), we tear down many walls and again have an inkling of God's intentions for the human family." Of course, at the bread counter, that is not the explicit intention as we come to the board and slice the bread. Nonetheless, even there we find a sacredness of the moment, and we find that a common humanity is shared. Nouwen continues, "Thus, the breaking of the bread . . . brings us into contact with people whose bodies and minds have been broken by oppression and torture and whose lives are being destroyed in the prisons of this world. This brings us into touch with men, women, and children to whom physical, mental, and spiritual beauty remains invisible due to lack of food and shelter. . . . These connections are indeed 'bread connections.'"[8]

In those places where we can visibly see the brokenness of the body and the spirit, we can offer what is possible for us to give. Those who are broken yet who do not reveal their own brokenness are also in need of the bread of connection about which Nouwen writes. First-time visitors who come to our congregations usually do not reveal what brings them to the congregation that day. However, a couple came to our congregation one Sunday and, after being introduced, the husband said he came because he had just been diagnosed with terminal cancer and was in need of a community in which to belong. It was unusual for someone to speak so truthfully at first meeting. But it is not unusual that people carry enormous burdens of brokenness in themselves. Attentive to those subtexts, the welcomer needs a listening heart so the various threads of a person's story might be heard.

The visual image of the bread being broken during the communion service is a symbol of the brokenness in our lives and in the world. When I have witnessed bread that was "sliced," I have been amused and somewhat chagrined when I reflected on the bread given out in the service. At the bread company, when we give out the free slice, we use a very sharp bread knife. When we slice a loaf of bread before we put it in the bag, we use a machine that makes equal pieces, about twenty-one slices per loaf. It is all so neat and tidy. When I use the phrase, "we break bread together" to describe what we do in the congregation, I have a very different image. Sliced or broken? When we use a sharp knife at the bread counter, there is a clean cut. When we break bread in the congregation, tearing pieces, the break is not smooth or clean. It is usually jagged; crumbs sometimes fall around. When my wife, who is a clergywoman, offers Holy Communion, she breaks and tears the loaf before giving the bread. She says the broken loaf is a metaphor for our life; the crumbs fall at our feet; the break is rough. That is what life is like sometimes.

In one congregation on Communion Sunday those who set things up had precut almost through the loaf of bread so that when the bread was "broken" it would still look like a clean cut, smooth, and with two equal pieces. Jesus' life and death, however, was anything but nice, presentable, and harmonious. As a symbol of him, the bread ought to be truly broken, not sliced. The broken bread acknowledges that people are welcome just as they are, imperfect and broken. That is the hospitality of the Spirit.

One of the gifts that a welcomer can offer to a visitor as well as to member is to be an empathetic presence. Even though they may have may be a brief encounter, the welcomer can be a companion on the journey with others. There are visitors who come to the church in need of healing or hope perhaps because they are homeless, recently in recovery, recently unemployed, or experiencing martial stress. Even if one cannot express such empathetic presence at the first encounter as the visitor enters, there are often opportunities in a conversation after the service or in the fellowship time. The value of a welcomer's spiritual attentiveness to a visitor is enormous. Likewise, for the welcomer it is a gift to be able to meet another person in their brokenness. Nouwen puts it this way, "My own experience with anguish has been that facing it and living it through is the way to healing. But I cannot do that on my own. I need someone to keep me standing in it, to assure me that there is peace beyond the anguish, life beyond death, and love beyond death. But I know now, at least, that attempting to avoid, repress, or escape the pain is like cutting off a limb that could be healed with proper attention."[9]

It is too much to ask that such encounters happen every Sunday, and it is unlikely that such empathy is sparked all the time. However, a welcomer can be someone who can be alongside others to help a visitor "standing in" whatever their brokenness may be. Paying attention to the possibilities of this gift given by the welcomer, and the gift that the visitor gives by being open, are essential elements in hospitality. "Standing in it" may include that a person cannot find the words to express her or his brokenness nor can the other person find the appropriate words to respond. Yet even a simple open-hearted greeting can be a beginning for the brokenness to find healing. The welcomer's own spiritual life can offer such a space. The grace of that space can be what one ordinary human being can offer another ordinary human being. The spiritual life of all can be nurtured in a congregation in particular through worship, small groups, mission projects, and pastoral care. Shaping that spiritual life can be named in the training that is offered anyone who is engaged in the ministry of hospitality. As a result, it is possible that a welcomer's spiritual depth will be experienced in those encounters where brokenness can be acknowledged.

GIVEN

Nouwen's first three words are "taken," "blessed," and "broken." The fourth word is "given." The bread is present, it is lifted up, blessed, broken in pieces, and then given out. Gunilla Norris writes, "And we also have known that we must share these gifts. They are not for us alone. Hoarded, they molder just as uneaten bread molders. We must share life, share bread with each other. We are given only so much time. And to make this time matter, in order to really live, we need to give, we need to receive. We need to love. Bread, life and love are fused in the soul of human experience."[10]

Reciprocity means giving and receiving. I enjoyed giving out the bread. I delighted in the encounters, which included giving my attention. I was touched by so many times I was allowed to give appropriate warmth. However, since a gift only becomes a gift when it is received, I came to understand that it was not possible for me to control how another person received what I offered at the bread counter. All I could do was offer it. Likewise in our congregations, all that we can do is offer the invitation to partake in the life of faith in the congregation, to engage in the worship, the fellowship, the education, the mission, and the welcoming of others to join in. The gift is only a potential until the person to whom it is offered accepts it. Yet whether or not the person accepts it as a gift, hospitality still needs to be offered.

While the giver receives the gift of the person who accepts what is given to him or her, the giver has to be wary of pride in the giving. "Sometimes it's more blessed to receive than to give, at least it takes more humility," wrote William Sloane Coffin.[11] I enjoyed giving out the bread, yet I found myself not as attentive to my own ability to receive in other contexts. Many people do not like to be on the receiving end. It takes humility to receive. At the bread company, I was the person who had the power to give. I chose the amount of bread to slice. I had the freedom to choose what bread might be available. I could even offer a cookie as a gift. I was the giver. I hoped to give my attitude of welcome and hospitality. What I received was a person's response of grateful reception. That made it a gift. Yet if I was the person receiving the bread would I be truly grateful? The spiritual truth for welcomers is to acknowledge her or his own dependence and need in being a person who receives a welcome or even a piece of bread. The image of baby birds feeding, of them receiving nourishment, comes to mind.

Have you ever witnessed a mother or father bird feeding their babies in the nest? The babies open their mouths to receive the food from the parent bird. A trustful receiving and a love-filled giving are happening. As people come forward for Holy Communion in a Christian congregation, many open their hands and some open their mouths ready to receive the bread. It is a trusting, vulnerable, place to be. They exhibit a willingness to receive.

The hunger for human connection was manifest as people came to the bread store for bread just as people come to the congregation. Giving the best welcome possible makes the encounter connecting. If a guest were to come to your home and you did not greet them, take their coat, invite them to make themselves comfortable, and offer them some refreshment, you would be considered rude and inhospitable. People come to our congregations as guests of our creating, redeeming, and sustaining God. As agents and instruments of this divine energy, we are to give guests the same gracious welcome we would give them if they came to our own home.

In the congregation, we are the living bread to each other. Our lives are broken open for each other as we feed one another and are fed with the blessing of the Spirit. Then we can give of ourselves in the service of the God who is host to us all. The next chapter suggests some ways of doing this, and, in the final one, I tell stories of such practices that continue to inspire me and that I hope will prompt you to tell and collect your own stories.

8

THE SCOPE OF THE MINISTRY OF HOSPITALITY

Love needs to be proved by action.

SAINT THERESE OF LISIEUX[1]

PRACTICALLY SPEAKING, HOW CAN WE BE LIVING BREAD TO EACH OTHER? How can we become good hosts in the way that God is host to all? The ministry of hospitality in a congregation will include these aspects:

- Invitation to the congregation's worship or one of the congregation's programs

- Welcome to any part of the congregation's activities

- Orientation to the congregation's faith and life

- A way to make a commitment to this congregation as a member

- A way to become incorporated into the life of the congregation in order to feel a sense of belonging

These aspects can overlap and do not necessarily follow any particular order. However, each of them can be attended to in a way that is appropriate for a congregation and will be authentic and of good quality.

INVITATION

Over the years we have come to realize that the best way for the invitation to be offered to others is personally. The advertising budget cannot hold a candle to the worth of a personal, verbal invitation to another person. Yet these days a congregation's informative and up-to-date website can be a very useful way to extend the invitation, too. The number of church visitors who check out the church on the web is increasing. Hearing about what the church is doing comes from those who are positively engaged in the congregation, and their own enthusiasm is contagious.

WELCOMING

A very good question to ask is "What if it works?" What if people do respond to the invitation and actually show up? This book has been focusing mainly on this aspect of the ministry of hospitality, the welcoming. Yet along with the conversation between the visitor and the welcomer, hopefully there will be an "Exploring Membership" time available for visitors to talk about what brought them to the congregation initially and what it is that has brought them back. This will also give them the opportunity to meet other members, as well as the minister and others who may also be exploring membership.

Along with the first welcoming encounters, we learned a variety of ways to follow up with visitors who came to the congregation in the first place. It may be by a telephone call or an e-mail or letter during that first week after they visit. In the follow-up telephone calls, the welcomers might learn new information from the visitor, such as what their experience of the church was like, what brought them to the congregation, what they are looking for in a congregation, or what particular questions they might have. Since in my congregation we have regular Exploring Membership sessions, visitors are invited to attend to learn more. In some congregations there is something to offer each visitor, such as a baked goodie or a coffee mug with the congregation's logo. This first encounter and the way we follow up on it are crucial to how a newcomer experiences our community.

ORIENTATION AND MEMBERSHIP/COMMITMENT

Congregations have a variety of formats to orient visitors. Some have a series of meetings a couple times a year and some have one luncheon every month with a time to join the congregation the following Sunday. Each congregation must find what is most appropriate for them. Having ways to gather those who are exploring membership is essential. In our congregation we call these orientation sessions "Exploring Membership."

We began by having two Exploring Membership gatherings quarterly, and those who subsequently decided to join the church did so during the New Member Sunday following. The invitations to these gatherings came from the names of visitors the welcomers had met, from the list of those who signed the pew pads during the worship service, or from the information sheets filled out by the visitors. The positive aspect of this approach was that we had enough time between gatherings to have a strong number of people who were interested. The down side is that it left too much time hanging between the times to join. So we decided to have one Exploring Membership luncheon per month following the service, and those persons who decide to join the church do so on the Sunday following the luncheon. Having that luncheon in the church has the advantages that we are able to offer those attending a tour of the church facilities without taking up much more of their time. It also gives more opportunities for people to join during the year. The downside is that many people are not ready to join the church that next Sunday when there is just one luncheon. Besides, today many people do not commit themselves right away. So we also tried gatherings to explore membership at the minister's home on a Sunday afternoon. The cozy atmosphere of the home setting was a draw. But the question remained of how often to have these meetings.

After several years we decided to have the Exploring Membership gatherings at the minister's home after Sunday worship on two consecutive Sundays, with the reception of new members in church occurring two weeks after the second New Member gatherings. These gatherings are on alternate months. Even more recently, we are considering having one Inquirer's Gathering/Exploring Membership gathering a month, with a New Member Sunday subsequently. It depends on the context of the congregation as to what the procedure will be. There are, of course, many different possible configurations of the Exploring Membership gatherings and the New Member Sundays, but typically their organization is the responsibility of a membership committee.

Attending a gathering at which one explores membership does not mean that that person will actually join. We are finding that many people are testing the waters and are less ready to commit (to the church or anything else) than in the past. Our experience is that many of those who do decide to join have already been part of some program or project, or are frequent worshipers at church. Since involvement leads to decision, the more opportunities there are for visitors and newcomers to participate in the life of the church, the better are the chances that they will commit and join.

INCORPORATION/BELONGING

In some congregations, once a person has joined, that person is on his or her own. It is the new member's responsibility, some say, to get to the point where he or she will say, "this is my church. I belong here." This is the goal of incorporation. There are many ways to achieve that goal. Our congregation's membership committee hosts semiannual get-togethers with newer members to check in and see how it is going for them. If a congregation is large, it can be intimidating for a new member to find her or his place in the life of the congregation. If the congregation is small, there may not be enough options for the new member to find a comfortable place. Either way, it is incumbent on the membership committee to provide ways for the newer members to find a place in which to offer their gifts through the ministry of the congregation as well as receive the gifts of the congregation so new members can continue their spiritual journey.

One congregation I know compiles a photo directory for everyone who wants to be in it. At that time the church also compiles a "Time and Interest Inventory" on which individuals list the myriad skills and gifts they would like to share through the congregation. This is a good way for the newer members as well as the longer time members to indicate where God may be leading them.

During the stewardship drive to raise money for the church's budget, inviting people to make a pledge of their finances and their time is another way to involve people. People on the boards, committees, and task forces of the church also keep their eyes and ears open for those who might be willing to participate in the church's elected positions and invite them to join.

The ministry of hospitality includes these dimensions: invitation, welcome, orientation, membership, and incorporation. Although the membership committee does not lead all of these. it is that committee's task to oversee their implementation.

Congregations are made of people. The longer one attends and gets involved, the more one finds people toward whom one gravitates and people one avoids. How differences are welcomed and worked through is what makes the community of faith a faithful community. The following section describes some ways of welcoming and working through difference to build faithful community.

GETTING TO KNOW AND REMEMBER THEIR NAMES

> God's love sets me free to enter into community with other people—even when the community is a very limited one and is not the total communion that my heart desires. Only when I live in communion with God can I live in a community that is not perfect. Only then can I love the other person and create a space in which we might be quite distant or very close, but we can still allow something new to be born—a child, friendship, joy, community, a space where strangers and guests can be received.[2]

I am realizing that when I can say the customer's name, he or she perks up. It is a basic human need to be known by name. That is one of the meanings of what christening or baptism is about in the Christian community, the naming of the child, the beloved one who is known by God. Therefore, as I say Justin, Greg, Mark, Alex, Ginny, or Reg the scene changes. The connection is begun.

Every congregation has to deal with knowing names, and many do it by wearing nametags. But are there nametags for everyone, or just for the elected officials of the congregation, just the ushers and welcomers, or just for the visitors? In one congregation, a different color coffee cup is offered to a visitor so as to let people know who the visitors are. Is there a photo directory of the congregation's members so people can put the faces with the names? There is not one best way to do it; however, being hospitable means knowing names. It does depend on the context of the congregation. I have seen smaller and larger congregations where there is one person or a couple of people who seem to remember everyone's name. They are the welcomers for the whole congregation. Hospitality oozes from them because they are genuinely interested in people and they have the gift of remembering names. Those are gifts that need to be discerned and then blessed.

If you cannot remember someone's name, it is far more hospitable to acknowledge that than avoid talking to that person. Approach the person and say, "I know we have met before, but I cannot recall your name. Please remind me and I'll try to do better next time." Then engage in conversation about whatever seems appropriate, and that might be a trigger to recall the person's name next time you meet. I have found it helpful on occasion to jot down a few notes in a notepad I keep in my pocket about the conversation and the person's name. It also helps to practice remembering, and to repeat, in your mind, the names of the people you meet. It does take time for me to remember names and to take the time to focus on how important names are.

MAKING TIME AND TAKING TIME

We are to deal with people with respect, whether that is in line for bread at the store or in the line for "bread" in the congregation. Whatever time we do have, if it is centered and focused, it can be rich and blessed. When it is rushed and scattered, the pulsating energy of life ebbs away.

A telltale sign of hospitality is having the time to be present with another person. Often when someone in my congregation has asked, "Do you have time to talk?" I have quipped, "time is all that I have." I don't think it is "wasting time" when we are invited to spend time with someone we love, someone we care about, and/or the one we come to know as God. It may mean not throwing time away but, rather, filling up time with an attentive presence that does not require or need any activity.

In my congregation, when all of the activities of setting up a welcome sign, having information available, and putting on a nametag before a service are done, then spacious time is available to be filled with the attitude of welcome. Not flitting around, but standing quietly. The welcomer can take a breath and choose an inner attitude of openness. Perhaps the welcomer can offer a silent prayer that God will grant all that the or she needs to be welcoming and to be ready to receive the blessing of those who enter. The welcomer might silently repeat a short verse from scripture, such as "those who wait upon God shall renew their strength," or "this is the day that God has made, let us rejoice and be glad in it." Taking the time may give time a quality of welcome.

OVERCOMING OUR FEARS

By taking the time, we also can often focus enough to overcome our own fears about talking with those we do not know. At the bread store, each person is given attention, but that is not always the case in our congregations. We need constant encouragement to reach out to those we do not know yet, although we know that some members are more gifted than others in this respect. It is not the smiley-faced welcomer that necessarily embodies hospitality, at least not the one with the plastered on smile. The smile that comes from a quiet place, a centered place, can truly welcome. That welcome can engender a connection with faith, a faith that lives with fear, a faith that is not overcome by fear.

"At the root of many less-than-welcoming attitudes toward others is fear," write Homan and Pratt. "If I am not at home in my own skin, enough to let someone share my space, how will I ever be able to look on the stranger with anything like kindness and welcome?"[3] Fears freeze hospitality. Embracing faith in the core of our life overcomes fears. It allows us to be at home in our own skin so as to offer hospitality to others.

In our congregations, the fears about finances and the number of members are real. Many years ago a clergyman said, "For many congregations it is about money and members, or bucks and bodies." Facing fears does not remove them. However it does allow finances and membership to be put in their rightful places. They are not the priorities that drive an authentic, growing congregation. As the faith deepens in a congregation, fear lessens. I have experienced the cries of babies that were months old. Their cries were not of the cries of hunger, the cries of pain, the cries of lack of attention, or the cries of tiredness. I am supposing that at least some of the cries were related to the anxieties of the parents who were holding the children. The parent's fears and their own uncertainties were translated into the baby's own awareness. If babies can pick up these signals, don't people in our congregations also pick them up? Our hospitality will not be hospitable if we are not ourselves grounded in the faith that can overcome fears. When we trust and live not by fear but by love embraced by the mystery that is beyond our understanding, then *all* is good; all the tears and all the joys are embraced together.

OFFERING STRENGTH BY BEING REAL

In our congregations it would be great if our welcomers could be prepared to listen deeply and to respond with a compassionate word and, if appropriate, even a word from the scripture. This is not to be a "fix" but a word of encouragement, not to cover over a person's situation or deny the tears that may come, but to offer strength.

"Life is good," is the phrase on some hats, sweatshirts, and tee shirts. "Is it?" I asked one man. "Yes it is," he exclaimed. "There are frustrations but still it is good." I have seen this phrase worn by many people. On occasion, I have seen the phrase lived as it is by a woman I know who is living with cancer.

Susan seemed a bit distracted as she came into the store, although the words on her sweatshirt proclaimed, "Life is good." "Is that true?" I asked. "Not really, but you don't have the time to hear about it." "Time is all that I have," I said, since there were no other customers in the store at that time. I stopped and looked right at her. "Well, I had surgery, abdominal surgery, and a hysterectomy. I was anemic. At the hospital, I got an infection, and I am still struggling with it. On top of that my dog ripped off one of his toenails, and my dad died last month." "Whew," I sighed, and was quiet. As she left, shaking my hand, I thought about how many people don't want to hear about those problems. It is easy to pass it off. But life is *not* always good. Like Humpty Dumpty, often many of the pieces of life are scattered, waiting to find ways to come back together, perhaps in a new way. But life, like Humpty Dumpty, does shatter us sometimes.

You know people who are battling some very difficult situations and conditions. When a person is receptive to that level of sharing, especially from an unexpected place and person, it can bring tears. I have thought that people carry unspoken grief and losses most days. It can make for a heavy walk and a long face. Whether in a bread store or a church, coming into a friendly and warm place where there is the free slice or a gracious welcome, might open a door for light to shine and sadness to be expressed and perhaps even relieved a little.

BUILDING COMMUNITY THROUGH COMMON STORIES

In her book *Untamed Hospitality*, Elizabeth Newman makes constant reference to the power of the story that a person lives out in her or his life. Without a story, however, a person is rootless and aimless, since the story a person chooses interprets her or his life. The essence of a person is "likely to be fragile and fragmented" and there is little meaning or purpose without a story. A person who is not placed in a context, who does not have a story, is vulnerable. Newman quotes Isak Dinesen "'all sorrows can be borne if you put them into a story or tell a story about them.' Dinesen implies that an unstoried self cannot bear sorrows."[4]

Persons who are part of a congregation have stories to tell, and it is stories that shape how people live. These are not stories they have made up, but stories that have carried them through their sorrows as well as their joys. Those who are exhibiting hospitality in the congregation are usually those who know they are part of a story that is larger than they are, and therefore they are able to invite others to share in that story, which includes joys and sorrows.

One Sunday when I was a welcomer in our congregation, a visitor hung around after the service. He was distraught, and I asked what was going on for him. He had just gone through a divorce and had moved to a new town. He was bereft. He had been part of a congregation in the past but did not now know where to go. After several more minutes, during which I gave him information about the congregation, programs that are available, and the name of the senior minister, who would be open to talking with him, I found myself asking if he would appreciate a prayer. Right there and right then. He said yes. So we held hands and I indicated that I would begin to pray and then would allow some quiet time if he would like to pray as well. I prayed. We were quiet. He prayed. It was a gift. Over the following weeks, I was looking for him but did not see him. He has the information about our congregation. We were able to connect through prayer. We blessed one another. And the journey continues.

The heart of hospitality is invitation—inviting others to experience the personal, communal, and social dimension of faith lived out. All we can do is invite; we cannot control the response but indeed have to surrender our control. Of course, a welcomer can invite someone more than once and in more than one way to participate in prayer or a program, attend the Exploring Membership gathering, or go to the fellowship time after the service. Persistence is a good quality of hospitality because when the person is ready to accept the invitation, the invitation will be received in a different way than if the person is not ready. Having the wisdom to know when is the best time to invite, or persist, or let go comes with practice.

Theological work that has helped me most with psychological insights such as these is the work of the late John Sanford, a Jungian analyst and an Episcopal priest. His writing about the biblical stories of Jacob, Joseph, Moses, and Adam and Eve has given me insight about the process of transformation that is available wherever we are, even at the bread counter or in our congregation. "[T]hese particular stories . . . concern the most important and fundamental process which goes on in a human life: the transformation of human beings from egocentric, unconscious persons to persons of wholeness, breadth of vision, and spiritual awareness."[5]

The final chapter contains some of the many stories of hospitality that inspire my practice and remind me of why faith communities have something to offer.

PART THREE | STORIES OF ENCOUNTER

9

THE STORIES

God made humans because God loves stories.

—ELIE WEISEL[1]

Liturgically, these stories of encounter with which I close act as a kind of Dismissal, a sending out into the world to do the work of God. I put them here to inspire, but also in hopes that you and your congregation will add stories of your own hospitable encounters by way of an ongoing conclusion to reading this book.

For me, these stories epitomize the movements that happen in encounter: sharing of ourselves; sharing happiness, tears, and joy; giving the "free slice" of grace; sharing our fears and faith; embodying the theology that enlivens us; offering prayer for the world nearby and far away; and finding ways to renew ourselves so that we can continue to offer the hospitality that is the grace and welcome of God.

The power of stories is underscored by Susan Gregg-Schroeder in this way. "People in an African village purchased a television set. For weeks all of the children, youth, and adults gathered around the television morning, afternoon, and night to watch the programs. Then after a couple of months, the villagers turned the television off and never used it again. A visitor to the village asked the chief, Why doesn't anyone watch television?' 'We have decided to listen to the storytellers,' the chief replied. 'Doesn't the television know more stories?' the visitor inquired. 'Yes,' the chief replied, 'but the storyteller knows me.'"[2]

I begin with a particularly apparent expression of who I am, what I believe, what I care about: the myriad bracelets that I wear daily. I hope you will know me a bit more through this expression as I believe I might be able to empathize with you were I to hear your stories.

SELF-REVELATORY CONNECTING: Bracelets As Symbols of Shared Struggles

At our best, we become Sabbath for one another. We are the emptiness, the day of rest. We become space, that our loved ones, the lost and sorrowful, may find rest in us.[3]

To love at all is to be vulnerable. Love anything, and your heart will certainly be wrung and possibly be broken. If you want to make sure of keeping it intact, you must give your heart to no one, not even to an animal. Wrap it carefully round with hobbies and little luxuries; avoid all entanglements; lock it up safe in the casket or coffin of your selfishness. But in that casket—safe, dark, motionless, airless—it will change. It will not be broken; it will become unbreakable, impenetrable, irredeemable.[4]

In connecting with people, there is always a balance between how much to share that is personal and how much to withhold or not disclose. The cliché is that we have two ears and one mouth so we ought to listen twice as much as we talk. In customer service, the focus is on the customer and not the staff person. However, the staff is not a cipher either. I think there needs to be some substance to the connection if possible and if it is appropriate. If the customer asks about me, I will share just enough to turn the conversation back to them. If there is going to be a connection, if there is going to be a spiritual dimension to the encounter, there have to be two persons present. Each person has to "show up." Present means engaged, authentic, and to some degree transparent.

Henri Nouwen spoke these words about living with human frailty and pain:

> The great mystery of God's love is that we are not asked to live as if we are not hurting, as if we are not broken. In fact, we are invited to recognize our brokenness as a brokenness in which we can come in touch with the unique way that God loves us. The great invitation is to live your brokenness under the blessing. I cannot take people's brokenness away and people cannot take my brokenness away. But how do you live in your brokenness? Do you live your brokenness under the blessing or under the curse? The great call of Jesus is to put your brokenness under the blessing.[5]

I have been wearing between eleven to thirteen silicone bracelets for several years. The first one was the yellow Livestrong bracelet, a fundraiser for cancer research reminding us of Lance Armstrong, who battled and survived cancer and had by 2008 won the Tour de France seven times. Noticing the many colored bracelets I now wear, one customer remarked, "You must support many causes." I said, "Yes, and I love the colors! But also each one reminds me of a particular person or situation."

When I worked at the counter, if a customer was actually interested in what the bracelets said, I would list them or would ask them to name a color and without looking at it, I would talk about it. I would say what it meant. The words on each of my bracelets are listed below with its corresponding concern or situation.

Livestrong—cancer prevention & research

Breathe—cystic fibrosis

Hold On—suicide prevention

Fortius Altius—(part of the motto for the Olympics)—I say it is "Higher Power" as in the twelve-step program.

Equality—equal rights for persons of all sexual orientations

Godstrong—a reference to Ephesians 6:1011, putting on the whole armor of God

Make a Difference—AIDS in Africa

The time is always right to do what is the right thing (Martin Luther King Jr.)—justice

Engineers without Borders—EWB-USA

Mind Matters BIAA—brain injury

Katrina—hurricane relief

Dalton Kerr Staystrong—keep the faith while living with a terminal cancer

Stroke—support for persons who have had a stroke

Silent Protest—speaking out against the Iraq war

Erase Hate—www.matthewshephard.org

NAMI—dedicated to improve the lives of individuals affected by mental illness

So for example, one day a woman asked, "What is that dark blue bracelet about?" "It says BREATHE and is about cystic fybrosis." "I have a blue one, but it is for lupus. One of my friends has lupus." "What is that?" "It is an autoimmune disease that attacks one's own organs. It goes after one in particular, which the disease treats as a foreign body." You never know what you might learn at the bread counter, I thought. The blue one I was wearing I got from a mother when I was visiting her daughter who had cystic fibrosis, a life-threatening lung disease.

The bracelet that reads "Hold On—We care at www.colies closet.org" (light blue) is about offering ways to prevent suicide through support and resources. It reminds me of my own brother's death by suicide and the unspeakable pain of those who face the suicide of a loved one. I have struggled with how hopeless a situation can become. I just don't know what it is really like for someone. I realize that some brain disorders may be treated with medication, and yet sometimes the doses don't meet the need. Major depression is a brain disorder that *may* lead to death by suicide. My work with NAMI, the

National Alliance on Mental Illness, has given me insight about this disease and ways to support those who experience it and their families.

The "Godstrong" (red bracelet) comes from a conversation with a twelve-year-old girl in the hospital. She wore it to remind her of the strength that she needed as she battled anorexia. The bracelet refers to Ephesians 6:10–11 from the New Testament. "Finally, be strong in the Lord and in strength of his power. Put on the whole armor of God so that you may be able to stand against the wiles of the devil." She was torn between the voices that wanted her to eat and be well and the voices that told her she was too fat and should not eat. She was wasting away and could die. She wanted the strength to win her battle to health.

The gray bracelet says, "Stroke." The stroke that I had when I was fifty years old affected my language center. I did not know my name nor could I speak or understand. It was speech therapy, mostly, that exercised my brain enough that I could recover speech and understanding. In addition, there was my loving wife and a faithful community of people who held me in prayer. The recognition of my name took three days, and after several months of therapy, I was able to remember how to make change for a quarter and to begin to use language again.[6]

All of these bracelets as well as the others that I have in my dresser drawer remind me of my connection with the humanness of people at points of their distress, at the end of their rope, or living with their acknowledged limitations. The bracelets gave me a way to connect with people at the counter, but more importantly they connect me with the cloud of witnesses who experience conditions about which these and other bracelets speak.

The ministry of Jean Vanier speaks of the vulnerabilities with which we live and where transformation happens. He is the founder of the L'Arche community, which has established communities around the world for persons, and their companions, who are living with developmental disabilities. He wrote,

I believe that we are all very broken in our capacity to relate. Human beings like power and to be admired and to be brilliant. When you start living with people with disabilities, you begin to discover a whole lot of things about yourself. Some are easy to live with, but others can make you climb the wall. Others can make you touch your own brokenness, your own poverty. To be human is that capacity to love which is the phenomenal reality that we can give life to people, we can transform people by our attentiveness, by our love, and they can transform us.[7]

Scratch the surface of anybody's life and you will find that person or someone close to that person is struggling with any one of these human conditions. Sharing these stories, I believe, weaves the tapestry of spirituality in our common humanity. We hear the blessings even as we live the brokenness. Bracelets can help us remember, communicate with each other, and offer financial help when possible. Wearing the bracelet is a sign of the courage, strength, and hope that may come in those difficult situations. It is a powerful way for us to connect with each other and to receive encouragement on our journey. It is an experience of hospitality of the spirit.

THE CONTAGION OF HAPPINESS

Let no one be discouraged by the belief there is nothing one man or one woman can do against the enormous array of the world's ills, against misery and ignorance, injustice and violence. . . . Few will have the greatness to bend history itself, but each of us can work to change a small portion of events, and in the total of all those acts will be written the history of our generation.[8]

I have read about a practice to build up one's "happiness." It suggests naming three good things that have happened during the day as you are about to go to sleep. Doing this for several weeks may change one's level of hope or may increase the hope that is already there. It may become contagious.

A provider said about the chef in a local restaurant, "he has an infectious personality and it's the secret for his success." The most successful business relationships begin with a passion for what you're doing and sharing that with people with whom you work. Where does that positive energy come from? Where does happiness come from? In a restaurant, it may be the food, and those with whom you work. In a congregation, it may come from the lively faith that is resident in the members and being engaged in faithful activities. Thus, in both settings, enthusiasm can be infectious.

When I greeted Joyce one morning with an exuberant exclamation, she said, "I love coming here each day!" "Why?" I asked. "Because," she responded, "this is the Land of the Happy People." I laughed. She continued, "There are so many coffee shops around here and I do not go there because they are not happy places. Here there are smiles and a welcome." It is great that it shows on a consistent basis.

One day a woman at the counter said to me, "You are so happy!" I took that as a positive comment. I indicated that I am not an optimist but I am a hopeful person. What is the difference? There are shadows and sadness where we live. We can point to the conflicts and wars in this world. As of writing this, the war in Iraq has not led to a stable situation. The Sudan genocide and the Palestine/Israel conflict continue to break our hearts because of the suffering of everyone in those lands. Add your own list of the atrocities and unspeakable torments that are inflicted on people where the ground is soaking up their blood. No, I am not optimistic; however, I am hopeful. As well, we know that if you just scratch the surface of almost everyone's life you will find fears and anxieties about illnesses, losses, pain, and suffering. Still, I am hopeful. For even in those global and personal situations compassion may come. Support can be offered.

When visitors come to the congregation, not only the welcomers but all the members can embody "contagious happiness." This experience needs to be present from when the visitors come into the congregation until they leave. The buoyancy of hope that comes from knowing the God who welcomes all is something we hope to make tangible. Nothing that is human is alien to us. This is not "smiley button Christianity." It is welcoming what is. It is hospitality.

In our congregations, when people come as visitors, they are checking things out. They are shopping around. They are looking at how things work. What do they see? How do people treat them and how do the members treat each other?

Just as in the bread store grumpy customer service spoils the delicious bread, in our congregations visitors are repelled by the few cold and unwelcoming people even if there are also warm and hospitable folk. "What if the neighbors and strangers among us look (at our congregation) and see squabbling and pettiness? What if they see a disjointed group of people who really aren't community at all? It's obvious that a little hospitality within the community is in order here, not the tea-and-cookies kind, but the kind that says, 'I'm going to listen to you and respect who you are.'"[9] Happiness is an inside job. It grows when there is respect and listening.

It is fun to be at the bread company since our enjoyment in giving and selling good bread is woven into the way we work. It is positive and it is energizing. People catch it. That goes for spirituality, too. It spreads by example.

A local college student said during my lunch break, "This is my second home." A second home, I thought, what does that mean? "Well, it is the smell of the baking bread. The place is mellow. There is a free slice of bread all the time and people are happy, the staff enjoys being here. It does not feel like a business." The same contagious attitude can be embodied in a congregation through the team of welcomers.

When joy is in the air and in the lives both of those who are in customer service and in our congregations, the vitality of life is tangible, the presence of the Holy Spirit is real. This leads to spontaneity and flexibility in what we do in the store and in the congregation.

THE FREE SLICE IS TANGIBLE GRACE
Abundant Bread

The fundamental philosophy of the Great Harvest Bread Company is to offer a hefty slice of free bread for everyone who comes in, even before they ask for it. It is available all the time and the staff is ready all the time to give the slice. There are people who buy four loaves of bread, there are those who buy a sandwich with chips and soda, and there are those who just are stopping by, running in and out, hankering for the warm slice with butter and/or honey, and there are the homeless guys whose hunger hangs on them like their baggy clothes. Each and every person is generously offered a free slice of bread.

No one has to buy anything to receive the slice. It is freely—gracefully—given. People who have a marketing penchant, of course, have said, "That is a very good way for people to buy. Have a taste and decide to buy the bread!" However it works, my experience has been that no guilt is created around the breadboard. "To buy or not to buy" is not the motto. "To sample or not to sample" is all it is.

When I slice the bread at the counter, I appreciate that I have the latitude to cut a large slice. One man smiled after I gave him his slice and said, "You give the thickest slices of bread of any bread company I have been in." That was a positive acclamation. Very few people ask for the slice to be made smaller! However, there are several who ask to have it cut it so they can share it with someone else. Most take it with thanks. I could have given a skimpy slice, of course, but that would not mesh with the attitude that I seek to bring to the counter, let alone show how to live with hospitality in the world.

Knowing we can give either a healthy slice or a slim slice of bread, I have realized that there are at least two attitudes that shape our lives. One is that there is not going to be enough of whatever it is that we think we need. That is an attitude of scarcity. The other is an attitude of abundance: the underlying trust that there will always be enough of what we need. To receive a skimpy, thin slice of bread may reinforce the scarcity attitude. The thick slice indicates that there will be enough. We want to err on the side of abundance rather than scarcity. This is a spiritual lesson that I witnessed at the breadboard every day.

Congregations that are growing usually have these three challenges: insufficient staff, a need for new programs, and a need for more money. Those congregations that can see these challenges as opportunities and live into those concerns with an attitude of grace and abundance will flourish. Those that see these issues as insurmountable obstacles will not.

There always seems to be enough bread at the bread company, always enough to offer the grace-filled slice! Is not the grace of God abundant? Isn't there not only enough to go around but always more? We are to choose abundance, not scarcity, as the way to live and grow.

Practicing Generosity to All in Need

"You have not lived a perfect day, even though you have earned your money, unless you have done something for someone who cannot repay you."[10]

At times, I have been ashamed of my attitude in the store toward people who are homeless. As we were closing the store one night in January, a couple came in. Each had on several layers of clothes. It was cold. The fragmented story they told was that they were driving to her family's home in the south. They were stuck in Boulder in a snowstorm, and the battery of their van was shot. They were wandering the city, enjoying the town, they said. When they learned that we regularly gave all the two-day old bread to a local agency, they asked if they could have some of it. They began by asking for a cinnamon roll, then two, and then we got up to ten. Then the oatmeal cookies. It started with two and then went to all of them, about twelve. The man said, "We could be Santa Claus and pass this along to others." They asked for a large black plastic bag and filled it up with the muffins, scones, rolls, and the cookies that were left at the end of our work day.

The Carriage House in our town is a center that assists homeless persons in finding employment and receiving referrals for mental health care and for drug rehabilitation. That night I was intending to take some of the food that was not going to be sold to that center. Was I going to take food from the two in front of me and give it to those that I would probably not see? The other items that had not sold that day would be put in bags for the local food share program.

The couple settled at one of the counters, drinking coffee and using their cell phone. Each was using the bathroom. The man was many years older than the women. She looked like an old time hippy and he looked like an old pothead, I thought to myself. What an attitude was growing in me! I assumed that they were hapless, scrounging for any food they could. I did not trust that they were going to give that food away. Here I was, living in a home with heat, running water, and electricity. I had a refrigerator in which to store food. The words of the prophet Isaiah came to me, "Is this not the fast that I choose. . . . Is it not to share your bread with the hungry and bring the homeless poor into your house?"[11] Isaiah's words are direct, I thought. Would this couple be out tonight in the cold? Is their van some protection? Do they need access to the local shelter? They are cogent. They do not seem to be mentally unbalanced. Would I invite them into my house?

As we continued to close the store for the night, I wrestled with my negative attitude toward these people whom I did not know. They finally began to put on the layers of clothes that they had removed when they first settled into the store. As they went out the door he said, "Thanks for your hospitality!" That is *the* word for customer service: hospitality. This couple reminded me of the grace of hospitality. My stingy and hardened spirit began to dissolve, although my heart continued to be disturbed throughout the night by the whole scene. It was not my job to judge what they did when they left the store, I realized. I had to accept they were doing the best they could.

For congregations seeking to be hospitable to persons who are homeless, some of whom are also dealing with a brain disorder (mental illness), a good resource is Craig Rennebohm's book *Souls in the Hands of a Tender God.* Having worked on the streets of Seattle for more than twenty years, this United Church of Christ clergyman has learned about homelessness and mental illness and ways that congregations can offer hospitality to persons experiencing either or both. As a special ministry, some members of a congregation may focus on this outreach. Rennebohm writes, "Out front (of our congregation), the reader board proclaims, 'All are welcome, come as you are,' but our ability to put that bold and basic principle into practice had a serious limitation when it came to the nearly 10 percent of us who are afflicted with major depression, bipolar disorder, schizophrenia, or other severe mental illness."[12] In our congregations, to embody the message of hospitality takes courage, imagination, compassion, and the willingness to understand. If welcome means only some are welcome but not all, then we have not lived into what the challenge and gift of hospitality means.

Our congregation practices hospitality by offering, in partnership with other congregations in our town, a free meal every month to persons who are homeless. Serving the meal and cleaning up after the meal are just a part of the gift. The larger gift for me is having the chance to listen to those who come for the meal, their stories, their hopes, and their thanks.

However, there are times when I just don't know what to do. One Sunday a person who was homeless came into the sanctuary. He was greeted and acknowledged. As people were leaving, he took out a hand made sign that said, "Hungry." One member told him that there is a free hot lunch at a local church every Sunday and that on that particular Sunday it was just a block away. He was encouraged to get a meal there. Indicating that he knew that the meal would not be served for an hour and he was hungry now, he persisted in holding the sign in the faces of those who were leaving. Another member offered to take him to the fellowship time, where there would be some food right then. He indicated that it would be too sweet for him and bad for his teeth. Exasperated, he was ushered to the street so as to go to the church where the lunch was being prepared. He resisted. Right then a member came along and gave the man with the sign some money. What is the hospitable thing to do in this situation? Ought I to have offered to take him to a local restaurant to get a meal? Having been taken in by so many people who wanted money, I was not going to hand him cash. What about finding out if there was food at the fellowship time that was not sweet? I was in a quandary and did not come up with a gracious response myself, while another member gave the man the money.

At the bread counter, I have also experienced my limitations. And while I can always do better at work, it is in my congregation that I can find the words of hope and forgiveness to actually do better. Being hospitable to those to whom I do not feel like being hospitable is difficult for me. There are those days when I pray that someone else will be welcoming, since I just cannot do it. The bread company, however, forces me to greet and wait on whoever is there in front of me, whether or not I come to like them. It is not about liking but about being present. It is not about being phony but about being gracious. It is not about being perfunctory but about knowing I am welcomed and so being able to welcome the other.

A middle-aged man was buying a loaf of bread when he noticed a man who seemed to be homeless. Both of the men were standing at the breadboard, wanting a slice of bread. The first man took his change and then gave me six dollars saying, "Give him a loaf of bread of whatever he wants." I took the money; the disheveled man took a loaf of bread. We all nodded to each other, and they each left with their bread.

Over and again, I have been a witness to such hospitality of others. It has caused me to notice the level of my own hospitality. Of course, I like to believe that since so many people come into the bread store and witness the free slice of bread that is offered to everyone, many people will catch the spirit of hospitality of that act and go and do likewise. There are those moments, however, when it smacks me right in the face that I am not living up to what I say I believe. Then I have remorse. The redemption usually comes when I act differently the next time.

This self-conscious attitude can deepen the quality of the connection between the staff and the customer. I can learn more from occasions that make me wince than when I just read about these "right" things to do. At least if I don't run away from those uncomfortable feelings, they might lead me eventually to be in a better place spiritually and emotionally. Perhaps that is why grace is needed most when I am not acting gracefully. I have learned through the twelve-step programs that acknowledging my own weaknesses and powerlessness can lead to a genuine strength that comes through a power greater than me.

Coffin writes, "Maybe it is the pain and not the peace of God that 'passes all understanding.'"[13] We know there is human pain in the world as a result of hunger, floods, hurricanes, and earthquakes, along with wars, the inhumanity of humans to each other, and abuse; all this and more point to the sufferings that people endure. Much of the suffering is beyond our understanding. There are also stories of pain and suffering in those who come into the store. We stand in the mystery. We do not have the time or usually the inclination to know more than a small portion of those stories. Yet when customer service staff is cognizant of the potential of those stories to be told, it can lead to some peace in the pain when the stories are told! In whatever way we get there, those who are engaged in the ministry of hospitality need to have delved into this well of inadequacy to find the yet deeper resources of strength to connect with people wherever they might be. It can be an encounter with grace.

Standing at the breadboard, the grace of it all takes my breath away once in a while. The grace of the free slice brings forth many of my attitudes about generosity and scarcity, my judgmental and open-hearted responses, and my inhospitality and my welcome. Encountering those who are homeless, typifying my own sense of not being at home in my own self at times, reminds me of my connection with others who seem less fortunate than me. Sharing food at the breadboard, I realize how fortunate we are to be able to have bread to give away and to sell, and that there are people who are willing to receive the gift and/or to buy. The ongoing encounters can remind me over and again of the grace that is so present and so available.

At the bread store, during business hours the doors are open, not locked. The staff is to be there with welcome and ways to engage. In congregations, during worship services in particular, the doors are open and many congregations have signs that say "welcome." But are the congregations open and are they welcoming? Are members prepared to respond to the needs of those who come to visit? Prepared to listen to their pain as well as joy?

TEARS AND JOY

Give your sorrow all the space and shelter in yourself that is its due, for if everyone bears [his or her] grief honestly and courageously, the sorrow that now fills the world will abate. But if you do not clear a decent shelter for your sorrow, and instead reserve most of the space inside you for hatred and thoughts of revenge—from which new sorrows will be born for others—then sorrow will never cease in this world and will multiply.[14]

In a review of the movie *The Diving Bell and the Butterfly*, John Petrakis writes, "The film suggests that regret and remorse are part of any existence, no matter how early or suddenly it ends, but that bursts of joy and gentle encounters are also part of the not-so-neatly wrapped package."[15] The true story is about a man who suffers a massive stroke that leaves him paralyzed except for the movement of one of his eyes. By this means of communication, he is able to write a book about his experience by dictating it to a scribe, one blink and one letter at a time.

The jumble of tears and joy wrack and bless our not so neatly wrapped human condition. The blend of the bane and the blessing of living are touched upon at the counter. There are, indeed, "bursts of joy and gentle encounters" at the counter. The context, the heart prepared to listen, the sometimes quirky way to respond to the phrases on someone's sweatshirt or hat, the visible clues in the way the customer comes into the store, as well as the energy that is swirling in the place together lend themselves to an encounter with gentle joy.

Sometimes tears do come at the counter. Barbara, a middle-aged woman, asked about how many bracelets I wear, noting all the varied colors. She said she wears the Livestrong one and has courage that she gets from her sons. "Well, you must have it," I said, "because you seemed happy as you came into the store." She had chosen some bread and the oatmeal cookies since her sons would love them. At that point, she began to break down. "I have been trying so hard to be happy. I have cancer. I was getting ready to run the Bolder Boulder (a 10K citizen's running race), and they said for only two hundred dollars more I could have a heart scan. Why not, I said. That is when they saw the tumor next to my heart. I had no symptoms. I was surprised. How can this be?" A pause. "The chemo is difficult," she said. "What about your spiritual strength?" I asked. "My friend takes me to church. It is a large church," she says, pausing to catch her breath. "I want to live. I want to see my sons married. I want to see my grandchildren." Another pause. "I will beat this!" she asserts, pausing again, then admits, "But I am afraid."

A phrase came to me at that point and I said, "'Love casts out fear.' You told me you have a lot of love from your sons. In addition, there is love in you. That makes fear fade. Courage means you can act in face of your fears and love will cast them out." "One of my sons moved here from New York to be near to me. I am so fortunate. From where is that phrase about fear?" I tell her it is from the Bible, from 1 John 4:18. She writes it down: "There is no fear in love, but perfect love casts out fear." When this truth is told, the tears of sorrow may turn to the tears of joy.

In our congregations it would be great if our welcomers could be prepared to listen deeply and to respond with a compassionate word, and if appropriate, even a word from scripture. This is not to be a "fix" but a word of encouragement, not to cover over a person's situation or deny the tears that may come, but to offer strength.

A woman came into the store one afternoon when there were no other customers. She looked tired and beaten down. I lifted up my arms and said, "Welcome." As she came to the breadboard I said, "Do you need a slice of bread? What about some water, which I could pour over your head?" She smiled and said, "I think I do need that." She walked to the shelves of bread and I came out from behind the counter and looked at the bread with her. "You seem a little down," I said. She said, "Yes, my daughter is stuck in Maine. She was coming home from Israel and I got a telephone call from the airline from her. Here it is September 11 and I am so worried that something has happened to her." She began to tear up. "It's thunderstorms in New York City that prevented her from landing there, where she was to transfer to a flight back to Denver. I am so nervous." I just stood there and breathed. She took a deep breath and went back to the breadboard. I offered her a piece of challah that we had made for the Jewish high holy days. After a while she said, "You made my day." I shook her hand and offered "shalom" as she left with a smile.

As you read these vignettes, you know people are battling some very difficult situations and conditions. When a person is receptive to that level of sharing, especially from an unexpected place and person, it can bring tears. I have thought that people carry unspoken grief and losses most days. It can make for a heavy walk and a long face. Whether coming into a bread store or a church, through authentic hospitality, one can tell one's story, express one's sadness, and perhaps even be relieved a little if for no other reason than that another human also lives the human story.

Our Christian story is one that reminds us that the love of God will not die and that, even though you may be knocked down by trials and tribulations, God will embrace you and lift you up again and again. "My brothers and sisters, whenever you face trails of any kind, consider it nothing but joy, because you know that the testing of your faith produces endurance; and let endurance have its full effect, so that you may be mature and complete, lacking in nothing."[16]

FEAR AND FAITH

"To be afraid is to behave as if the truth were not true."[17]

Spirituality is living in face of fears with love, for love casts out fear. Spirituality makes me part of a larger arena, a larger context. It allows the gift of being part of a power that is greater than I am, that is not dependent on the self. Our little self is significant because we are connected with this larger Self or mystery. In light of this connection, we do not fear. Of course, the Great Harvest Bread Company is not my business. It is not the center of who I am. Rather, the living relationship that I have with the transcendent God who is immanent in life and in me makes me who I am. Connection with God removes fear and brings spiritual strength—at least that is my quest.

Fear and trust exist in themes in our daily living. Living out of one or the other will shape what happens in our daily life. Jim Forbes, former senior minister of the Riverside Church in New York City used the image of a puzzle in a way that helped me. Each of us, he suggested, is one small piece of the large puzzle. Our piece, our experience, fits somewhere. It has a place. I might not see the whole puzzle, but I will trust that God does. As I trust that truth, I will not fear. I will trust the One's creative love that weaves all things together. Romans 8:28 comes to mind: "All things work together for good for those who love God and are called according to God's purpose." When I am in the flow of the divine energy, everything does work together. There is life, and even when the hardships come, I know that there is a place for those difficulties since everything does work together, somehow.

THEOLOGY

Most of us have to taste our need in a fierce sort of way before our hungers jar us into turning our lives over to God. . . . In the Divine Arms we become less demanding and more like the One who holds us. Then we experience new hungers. We hunger and thirst for justice, for goodness and holiness. We hunger for what is right. We hunger to be saints. Most of us are not nearly hungry enough for the things that really matter. That's why it is so good for us to feel a gnawing in our guts.[18]

The themes of theological talk, truth-telling, and character formation come up at the counter but of course are also told in congregations.

Theological Talk

You can see what is in people's faces. The stress, the depletion, the expectancy, the enjoyment of a place with bustling energy, the delight of smelling baking bread, and/or a personal greeting at the breadboard. The encounter with a customer may lead to a good news story, a humdrum moment, an enervating or an energizing experience. The connection that is made with someone makes that person realize that she or he is seen, is important, and is acknowledged as a human being. While we might not use the word "God" explicitly, God is prevalent in our encounters.

Tina from our congregation has come to the bread store several times. It always seemed to be that when she did we got involved in some kind of theological talk. On one occasion she wanted to recall a particular word that she was not able to remember. "It is when you are filled up with awe, wonder, and encouragement," she said. "Like when God comes into your life. I know God is in me and I know the Holy Spirit is present and alive. I know Jesus, the human being, was real. However, the Jesus who is God I just don't get. I have been working on that. What was that word that I can't remember?" I offered, "Was it incarnation? Transcendent? Immanent? Epiphany?" "It had been used in one of the sermons I heard a couple weeks ago," she said. We were stymied. We paused. Then like a flash, a word came to me. "Numinous," I said. "That's it!" she replied. Numinous describes a sacred, holy experience when the veil is taken away and you are face to face with the power of the Holy and the ineffable.

One day, John recounted a blizzard of many years ago here in Colorado. "That included the Front Range, especially Boulder," he said. We heard about local people's struggles with the snow and about how incredibly long the snow was on the ground. It looked as if the record was almost going to be set during the winter of '06–'07. John remarked, "I was not anxious or upset about this. Of course, plans change; I had feelings of being out of control; but the word that came to me was 'surrender.'" What a great word, I thought. "However, you need to know the difference between giving up or giving in and surrendering," I said. "As Reinhold Niebuhr reminds us, have the wisdom to know that difference:

> *God, give us grace to accept with serenity*
> *the things that cannot be changed,*
> *courage to change the things*
> *that should be changed,*
> *and the wisdom to distinguish*
> *the one from the other.*[19]

This is a motto that is used in many twelve-step programs such as Alcoholics Anonymous. The word "surrender" is a word that has power and strength. Yielding may lead to a new way of engaging with whatever comes one's way. Surrender underscores what I cannot control. If I continue to fight whatever that is, it may break me. To yield to it may bring a renewed strength. Knowing the difference is a spiritual discipline that leads to a richer life. I said in the last chapter that the heart of congregational hospitality is invitation: inviting others to experience the personal, communal, and social dimension of faith lived out. All we can do is invite and then surrender our control and await the response of the person we have invited.

I know that the Great Harvest Bread Company is not a church, nor a synagogue, nor a mosque, nor a Buddhist meditation room. Yet hospitable interactions there do often embody love, God, and neighbor. Brian is a regular customer. He had some mental illness, and some had said that he was homeless. He was bright. He came in at least once a week for bags, a sandwich, cups, and a cookie. I said that I was going to New York City. "What will you doing there?" he asked. "Running a half marathon," I said, adding that I had lived there some years ago. "What did you do there?" "I am an ordained minister." "What church?" "The UCC." "I know them," he said. "They are Open and Affirming. They do good things. They reach out to the marginalized." I was moved to hear this message from one who was himself looked on as marginalized and who knew where he could be welcomed and included.

Truth-telling

Coffin writes, "Compassion without confrontation is hopelessly sentimental."[20] I wonder how I can be direct and confrontational if all the customer really wants is a free slice of bread. Can one both speak the truth *and* sell bread? It seems weird to think that there may be a prophetic witness in the business of selling bread.

If the goal is to sell the bread, then whatever gets in the way of that sale is antithetical to the business. Does customer service warrant "truth-telling" if that gets in the way of selling bread? Are ethics and customer service opposites? Most customer service advisors will admonish us not to argue with our customers. They warn us that customer service staff will never win an argument with a customer. There is a truth in that. "The customer is always right" is an old adage taught to salespeople. Yet there are times, I believe, when speaking the truth is the only way out, as well as the only way through.

This dilemma needs to be acknowledged unless the banality of hospitality thwarts an authentic encounter. Newman notes, "a sentimental, 'nice' hospitality easily coincides with a kind of self-blindness and an inability to speak the truth . . . it is precisely hospitality without truth that causes us to reduce hospitality to a bland niceness."[21] Throughout this book, I have sought to emphasize a hospitality that is anything but banal, anything but bland. Of course, it does not need to be brutal or brash either, just genuine. Finding the ways to speak the truth so that it does not come off as sour grapes or go to the jugular or be so blunted that no one realizes that you are speaking the truth at all is a practice that can be developed. Whether or not there is a strong relationship already present, when the situation calls for a truthful word to be spoken it ought to be spoken. Most people will pick up on the frozen smiles, smarmy charm, and blandness in conversations that will signal that genuine hospitality is not being offered. It is not real. "If we want to go deeper, however, desiring that as God's people we will grow together toward maturity, we must care enough to confront."[22] Speaking truthfully is hospitable.

In the process of one customer buying a sandwich, a conversation came up about the scandals at the local university concerning sexual harassment in the football program. He became dismissive of those women who were pressing a rape case against the school, indicating that he knew that it was a fabrication by the women. I bit my tongue, because one of the issues that concerns me is violence against women. I wanted to say that the prevalence of abuse of women is widespread, and it is wrong. I wanted to say that it would be better to understand the complex issues of a male-dominated culture in which women are violated than to be dismissive about an instance in which women have been accused of lying while they are seeking to speak their truth. But I did not. I was silent. As a consequence, I was sorry that I didn't speak the truth that I felt.

In my work with congregations, I remember a phrase attributed to Russell Baker. He said, "The old definition of the press's duty held that it was supposed to comfort the afflicted and afflict the comfortable."[23] If the words of love and justice are to live, they must live in the workplace, not just in services in congregations, in education classes, and weekly Bible study. I believe that if it is called for, and if there is a context in which it makes sense, and if there is even a modicum of a relationship, then a word spoken truthfully ought to be spoken, even if that is a hard bit of truth. It may seem confrontational, but such a word can be spoken out of compassion without judgment. Otherwise, the maudlin sentimentalism of blandness will cover whatever is truly human. I hope to do better myself.

The same goes in our congregations. Speaking a word that might make the situation uncomfortable needs to be done in an appropriate context and spoken with clarity and without acrimony. "Respect for the people's word need not mean approval for whatever they say. Any criticism becomes constructive when based on a fundamental attitude of respect and listening."[24] In the narthex of the congregation, if someone is bringing in a cup of coffee (which has happened), a gentle reminder that he or she could perhaps finish it outside is appropriate. When a touchy subject was brought up after a service regarding a building project in the community that I favored and another member did not, we were able to be clear about our positions, although neither of us changed our minds. When a discussion ensued about the renovation in the sanctuary, there was much heat. I clearly was in favor of the plans and one person in particular was not. However, it became clear to me that the disagreement was not about the issue itself but was colored by a previous issue that we were not talking about. That clouded the conversation. All I could do at that point was to state where I was and then to listen, since arguing would not lead to a resolution. Because of that "other issue," however, hospitality was thwarted. Since then it has been nigh impossible for graciousness to prevail in relationship with this person. It is only when the real issues can be told truthfully that healing can come.

Character Formation

John Ruskin wrote, "The primary reward for human toil is not what you get for it, but what you become by it."[25] In ethical theory, character (the person) is a central ingredient in the decision-making process.

I ask myself, "What am I becoming by what I do at work?" What forms my character comes, in part, from how I use my energy in the work that I do. At the bread store, I wonder if I am becoming joyful, compassionate, pained, amazed, empathetic, bored, weary, present, or distant because of what I am doing. Even in unconscious ways, what I am doing reveals my character that is being formed. How much better would it be if I were more conscious of what I do in order to train myself to be the person that I ought to be. By paying attention to our routine ways of acting, we see habits that are forming us. As we become more astute about how we behave, we become more aware of how we can relate with others more clearly and directly. Because of that consciousness, we also become more aware of the actions of other persons in customer service as well as in our congregations.

Encounters at the counter reveal the character of those who tell their stories. The man who shared the word "surrender," who seeks serenity; the woman battling cancer who needs courage; and the man who struggles with forgiveness—each bring an openness to the moment. We are humans hungry for bread, sustenance without which we would die. We are humans longing for human connection without which we would spiritually die. These encounters may include the possibility of deeper connections revealing our character as well as forming it by the ways we respond.

PRAYER

In the previous chapter I mentioned connecting through shared prayer with a visitor to our congregation who was newly divorced and new to town. Even though I did not see the man return, the moment of prayer was a gift for us both. The hospitality of welcome means there is no ulterior motive. It is what it is. Acknowledgement and connection. Prayer is what it is, as well. Though I had hoped that the man with whom I had prayed might find his spiritual home with us, that was not the reason for the prayer. Prayer was the response to having listened him into speech. Prayer is one way to connect with each other and with God. It would be helpful if our welcomers would be people of prayer.

St. Augustine wrote that prayer is a stammering after God. Eloquence is not the goal of prayer, although eloquence usually arises when the prayer comes from the heart. Words or even the rich fullness of quiet prayer can speak volumes if the person praying is simply seeking to offer prayer. In our congregations people could be available to offer prayers with those who are seeking prayer either before or after the service. Is it too much to ask the welcomers in our congregation to pray if the need arises? Could they at least direct those who are seeking for prayer to someone who will pray with them? In our monthly membership meetings, the responsibility for opening and ending with prayer is given to different members so they can learn about praying and pray aloud with others. Fostering a prayerful attitude is a good thing for welcomers even if they are not the ones to offer prayer with those who may welcome it. In many of our meetings, there is a time for spontaneous prayer. This reminds those who do speak as well as those who don't that being in the presence of God in prayer is prayer itself.

RENEWING YOUR RESOURCES FOR HOSPITALITY

Burnout can happen when routine no longer replenishes. And it happens even in our ways of being hospitable. When it does, change things up. Take a break. Read a book. Take a walk. Eat lunch outside. Watch people, especially children. Sit some place different each lunch break. Take a slightly different route to or from work. There are ways to keep a renewed spirit alive as one goes back to work at the counter, besides first putting work in its proper place in your life. Although I have learned that I must not give work the value and the importance that it cannot in fact give back to me, I have come to know the place of work in my life. It is what it is. My work is not the heart of who I really am.

In Thornton Wilder's play *Our Town*, Emily asks, "Do any human beings ever realize life while they live it . . . every, every minute?" The stage manager responds, "No . . . the saints and poets maybe, they do, some."[26] At the counter, I am neither a poet nor a saint. Occasionally I do feel that I am "poetry in motion," as things get very busy.

However, in the routine of the day, the sweetness of life may ebb and the poetic bliss of seeing the wonder of life may wane. It is at those moments when we realize the beauty of life, that Spirit does renew us.

There is a story of a sailing ship that ran aground on the shoals off the South American coast. As the days went by, the crew exhausted their supply of potable water. A passing ship signaled this message: "Lower the buckets where you are." The crew didn't understand, didn't follow the signal's suggestion, and eventually died for lack of water. If they had lowered their buckets into the ocean, they would have learned that it was fresh water! They did not know that they were close enough to its mouth for the fresh water of the Amazon River to surround them. There are signs of hope right where you are. Renewing energies are present and available. They can be embraced here and now. Drawing on the sources of energy that are present brings even more energy. That is how it works.

Anaïs Nin has said, "We don't see the way the world is; we see the world the way we are."[27] What shapes our particular worlds? Cancer scans; loss of a job; birth of a baby; a new relationship; remembrance of a loved one who has died; a new adventure; or a struggling child. At work and in the congregation, when there is faith that the bucket that one lowers will draw up the refreshment of the Spirit, the encounter is renewing.

As a welcomer in a congregation reaches out to extend hospitality, he or she understands that it is the Spirit that undergirds and surrounds the encounter. Energy comes from an affirmation of the presence of the Spirit at work. Even when the welcomer extends that welcome over and over again, it does not lead to burnout, since it is the energy of the Spirit that is connecting people to each other. It is not forced. It is a flow.

In *Ministry Burnout*, John Sanford describes a mountain lake that became stagnant. In order for a lake to be fresh and alive, there must be a source of water coming into it, as well as a way for the water to leave.[28] If there is no action, no movement of energy in our lives, and if there is no source for renewing the energy, like the lake we can become stagnant. Seeing the inlet and the output in our own lives can make us aware of how to pay attention to our own renewal. This image can help members of congregations see the give and take of activities and information that can be renewing. Shutting down leads to stagnation. Opening up may lead to connection. Not taking in the new can petrify. Giving the energy of attention can fortify.

Sanford likewise writes about a well at his family's cabin in New Hampshire. After many years of absence, he returned to the cabin to recall his time there. Among the memories was one of the fresh, cold water that his family pumped by hand from the outdoor well. Many years later when he tried to get water from it, he realized the well was dry. He did not understand. Talking to some old-timers in the town, he learned that the way that the water would fill up the well was through many tributaries bringing in the water. As long as the water was being brought up, the tributaries would continue to fill up the well. When the well was not used for a long time, small pieces of dirt slowly clogged up the tributaries, which prevented the water from coming in. Voilà! After time, no water at all.[29] The renewing resources are available, but they have to be drawn upon regularly in order for our spirits to be replenished.

The renewing resources for our life are available in our congregations. Congregants are invited to pray, in a prayer group or individually; to learn to practice meditation and centering prayer; to sing in a choir or with heartfelt voice in the congregation; to read spiritually enriching books and be disciplined in reading the scriptures; to listen deeply to others to discern the ways that the Spirit is moving; to walk the labyrinth; or to use any form of spiritual discipline that helps draw them closer to the heart of God. In scripture our God is likened to "living water," a well that will never run dry. We must keep our own pumps primed in order to stay spiritually alive and be truly hospitable.

EPILOGUE | And the Blessing . . .

MY EXPERIENCE AT THE GREAT HARVEST BREAD COMPANY HAS GIVEN me ways to practice hospitality in my congregation. When we are able to discern the spirituality of all we say and do, we will enter any encounter with greater confidence. When we pay attention and acknowledge the uniqueness of the other person, we will be more affirming. When we have the compassion and the openness to welcome both the struggles and the delights of life, we will be present to others. When we have the courage to speak truth with love and listen to the truth spoken to us, we will experience integrity. When we can listen deeply and receive the stories of others, we will know connection. When the faith story that we hold infuses our way of being in the world, we will see the possibilities for new life wherever it is emerging. These are ways that hospitality comes alive and is authentic.

Some people have a natural knack for hospitality. Although it would be wise to discern who in your congregation has this gift and recruit them to be official welcomers, others can also learn to extend a genuine welcome. The eventual goal is for everyone in the congregation intentionally and then naturally to practice connecting with others. It is true that, as our spirituality deepens, our hospitality increases. It is also true that as we become more conscious and focused on extending hospitality, our spirituality will deepen. My encounters at the counter have created a world of meaning and hope as I have heard stories and shared them.

Congregations have stories that are yet to be told and connections yet to be made. I hope the learnings from the breadboard will encourage you as you develop an intentional ministry of hospitality in your congregation. It will be exciting. It will be enriching. It will be a blessing.

NOTES

INTRODUCTION

1. Romans 12:13b.

2. Arthur Sutherland, *I Was a Stranger: A Christian Theology of Hospitality* (Nashville: Abingdon Press, 2006), 79.

CHAPTER 1. SHOWING YOUR SPIRITUALITY IN YOUR HOSPITALITY

1. Peter Duncan Gilbert, "Spirituality and Mental Health: A Very Preliminary Overview," *Current Opinion in Psychiatry* 20(6) (2007): 594–98, http://www.medscape.com/viewarticle/564898, accessed June 25, 2009.

2. Henri Nouwen, *Turn My Mourning into Dancing* (Nashville: W Publishing, 2001), 48.

3. Daniel Homan, OSB, and Lonni Collins Pratt, *Radical Hospitality: Benedict's Way of Love* (Brewster, Mass.: Paraclete Press, 2002), 110.

4. Nouwen, *Mourning into Dancing*, 43.

5. Ibid., 97.

6. Homan and Pratt, *Radical Hospitality*, 35.

7. Gary Ezzo and Anne Marie Ezzo, "Toddlers—The Neurological Boundaries of Learning," *Growing Families International* (Copyright 2001–2004), http://www.gfi.org/java/jsp/article40.htm, accessed June 25, 2009.

8. Homan and Pratt, *Radical Hospitality*, 179.

9. Ibid., 189.

10. Danny Meyer, *Setting the Table: The Transforming Power of Hospitality in Business* (New York: HarperCollins, 2006), 66.

11. Ibid., 143.

12. Ibid., 145.

13. *Left-Handed Fastballers: Scouting and Training America's Grass-Roots Leaders*, report based on a study for the Ford Foundation conducted by David Nevin (New York, August 1981), 97.

14. Kris Thompson, quoted in Ellen Simon "Employers Looking for Ms., Mr. Congeniality," Associated Press, http://www.seattlepi.com/business /340162_congenial19.html.

15. William Sloan Coffin, *Letters to a Young Doubter* (Louisville: Westminster John Knox Press, 2005), 27.

Chapter 2: Making Your Encounters Count

1. Frederick Buechner, from *Secrets in the Dark: A Life in Sermons*, quoted on *God's Politics*, blog, "Voice of the Day," http://blog.beliefnet.com/god-spolitics/2007/07, accessed July 12, 2007.

2. *Webster's New Universal Dictionary* (New York: Simon and Schuster, 1979), 598.

3. Ibid., 1656.

4. E. M. Forster, *Howard's End* (New York: Penguin Group, 2002), chapter 22, 187.

5. Meyer, *Setting the Table*, 79.

6. Wikipedia definitions for "anima" and "animus."

7. Coffin, *Letters*, 42–43.

8. Susan Heathfield, "Listen with Your Eyes: Tips for Understanding Nonverbal Communication," About.com: Human Resources, http://humanresources.about.com/od/interpersonalcommunicatio1/a/nonverbal_com.htm, accessed June 29, 2008.

9. Homan and Pratt, *Radical Hospitality*, 203.

10. Nelle Morton, *The Journey Is Home* (Boston: Beacon Press, 1985), 128.

11. Harriet McBryde Johnson, *Too Late to Die Young: Nearly True Tales from a Life* (New York: Henry Holt, 2005), 253–54.

12. Alan Johnson, "When Listening Also Hurts!" in the National Hospice and Palliative Care Organization's *Newsline Insights*, "Linking Hands, Linking Hearts: Caring for Seriously Ill Children and their Grieving Families" (March 2004): 51.

13. Gospel of Thomas, 45.30–33, in *The Nag Hammadi Library* (New York, 1977), 126.

14. Nouwen, *Mourning into Dancing*, 67.

15. Adrienne Rich, from "The Dream of a Common Language," in *The Fact of a Doorframe: Selected Poems 1950–2001*, (New York: W.W. Norton, 2002), 167.

16. Nouwen, *Mourning into Dancing*, 69.

17. Homan and Pratt, *Radical Hospitality*, 139.

18. Ibid., 131.

19. Nouwen, *Mourning into Dancing*, 82.

20. Elizabeth Newman, *Untamed Hospitality: Welcoming God and Other Strangers* (Ada, Mich.: Baker Publishing, 2007)175.

21. Nouwen, *Mourning into Dancing*, 75.

22. Ibid.

23. Ibid.

24. Meyer, *Setting the Table*, 244.

25. H. Richard Niebuhr, *The Purpose of the Church and its Ministry* (New York: Harper and Row, 1956), 27.

Chapter 3: Making Hospitality Come Alive

1. Joan Chittister, from *Wisdom Distilled from the Daily*, quoted on *God's Politics*, blog, "Voice of the Day," http://blog.beliefnet.com/godspolitics/2007/09, accessed 17 September 2007.

2. Paul J. Carlson and Peter S. Hawkins, eds., *Listening for God* (Minneapolis: Augsburg Fortress, 1994), 114.

3. Homan and Pratt, *Radical Hospitality*, 109.

4. Meyer, *Setting the Table*, 90.

5. Ibid.

6. Michele Hershberger, *A Christian View of Hospitality: Expecting Surprises* (Scottdale, Pa.: Herald Press, 1999), 15–16.

7. Matthew 24:42.

8. Meyer, *Setting the Table*, 145.

9. D. H. Lawrence, "We Are Transmitters," http://www.poemhunter.com/poem/we-are-transmitters/, accessed June 30, 2009.

10. Meyer, *Setting the Table*, 78.

11. A quite dense theological book that added depth and power to my faith is Alan Lewis's *Between Cross and Resurrection: The Theology of Holy Saturday* (Grand Rapids: Eerdmans, 2001). In this book Lewis explores the significance of the silence and the godforsakenness of the day between Good Friday and Easter. While this rings so true as he describes the divine presence-in-the-absence on that day, it also highlights "the self-abandoning love" (page 116) that is the call for all who are Christian. Delving into this theological thinking has shaped the way that I have come to understand the quality of hospitality that is truly Christian.

Chapter 4: Learning from Customer Service in Other Businesses

1. Steve Lopez, *The Soloist* (New York: Berkley Books, 2008), 10. In the encounter among Mr. Lopez, the journalist, and Mr. Ayers, a person who is a musician living with schizophrenia, the story unfolds over a couple of years. In the movie *The Soloist*, Mr. Lopez's on-call doctor says, "Relationship is primary. It is possible to cause seemingly biochemical changes through human emotional involvement. You literally have changed his chemistry by being his friend" (page 210). Encounters have positive impacts.

2. Newman, *Untamed Hospitality*, 91.

3. Meyer, *Setting the Table*, 67.
4. Ibid.
5. Homan and Pratt, *Radical Hospitality*, 132.

CHAPTER 5: TRAINING PEOPLE FOR YOUR SETTING

1. Patrick Lencioni, *The Five Dysfunctions of a Team* (San Francisco: Jossey-Bass, 2002), 195.
2. Corinthians 15:7.
3. Meyer, *Setting the Table*, 241.
4. Ibid., 248.
5. Ibid., 264.
6. Ibid., 267.
7. Ibid., 268.
8. Ibid.
9. Ibid., 270.

CHAPTER 6: CREATING CONTINUITY THROUGH STORIES OF HOSPITALITY

1. Barbara Kimes Myers, *Young Children and Spirituality*, quoted on *God's Politics*, blog, "Voice of the Day," http://blog.beliefnet.com/godspolitics /2008/05, accessed May 26, 2008.

CHAPTER 7: OFFERING THE BREAD OF LIFE

1. Henri Nouwen, *Life of the Beloved* (New York: Crossroad, 1992), 48–49.
2. Ibid., 51.
3. Ibid., 53.
4. Gunilla Norris, *Becoming Bread: Embracing the Spiritual in the Everyday* (Mahwah, N.J.: HiddenSpring, 1993), 3.
5. Nouwen, *Life of the Beloved*, 69.
6. Ibid., 69–70.
7. Ernest Kurtz and Katherine Ketcham, *The Spirituality of Imperfection* (New York: Bantam Books, 1992), 5.
8. Henri Nouwen, *The Only Necessary Thing* (New York: Crossroad, 1999), 176–77, reprinted from *Compassion* by Donald P. McNeill, Douglas A. Morrison, and Henri Nouwen (New York: Doubleday, 1982). Used by permission of Doubleday, a division of Random House, Inc.
9. Nouwen, *Life of the Beloved*, 95.
10. Norris, *Becoming Bread*, 3–4.
11. Coffin, *Letters*, 14.

CHAPTER 8: THE SCOPE OF THE MINISTRY OF HOSPITALITY

1. Saint Therese of Lisieux, *Story of a Soul,* quoted on *God's Politics,* blog, "Voice of the Day," http://blog.beliefnet.com/godspolitics/2009/02, accessed February 4, 2009.

2. Henri Nouwen, from a lecture at Scaritt-Bennett Center, quoted on *God's Politics,* blog, "Voice of the Day," http://blog.beliefnet.com/godspolitics 2008, accessed February 14, 2008.

3. Homan and Pratt, *Radical Hospitality,* 76.

4. Newman, *Untamed Hospitality,* 37.

5. John A. Sanford, *The Man Who Wrestled with God: Light from the Old Testament on the Psychology of Individuation* (New York: Paulist Press, 1974), 4. John Sanford's trenchant work is a combination of biblical and psychological wisdom. It is through the lens of his work that I have looked at the glimpses of transformation at the bread counter. There are occasions for this grace to surprise us. Without such stories about which Sanford writes, our own stories, even shards of them, would not be as enriched, ennobled, and encouraged.

CHAPTER 9: THE STORIES

1. Elie Wiesel, *The Gates of the Forest* (New York: Holt, Rinehart, and Winston, 1966). Weisel reached this conclusion based on a Chasidic tale of the Rabbi Israel Baal Shem-Tov about a succession of rabbis who, over time and generations, lose the exact words and ritual of intercession until the last rabbi knows only the story of the words and ritual—but it is sufficient for the intercession to God.

2. Susan Gregg-Schroeder, *In the Shadow of God's Wings: Grace in the Midst of Depression* (Nashville: Upper Room Books, 1977), 11.

3. Wayne Muller, from *Sabbatical,* quoted in *How Shall We Live,* by Joan Chittister. http://blog.beliefnet.com/godspolitics/2007/08, accessed August 7, 2007.

4. C. S. Lewis, from *The Four Loves,* quoted on *God's Politics,* blog, "Voice of the Day," http://blog.beliefnet.com/godspolitics/2007/11, accessed November 29, 2007.

5. Henri Nouwen, from a lecture at Scaritt-Bennett Center, quoted on *God's Politics,* blog, "Voice of the Day," http://blog.beliefnet.com/godspolitics /2007/10, accessed October 2, 2007.

6. Through the stroke I have been taught yet again about gratitude. During a conversation with Henri Nouwen just after the stroke, he said, "If you live with this stroke with gratitude, it will bring you closer to God. If you live this stroke with bitterness it will lead you away from God." Reflecting on

this experience, I wrote, "Over the years, I sensed that the self that I had come to know following the stroke was essentially deeper than all that I could do, more than I could say or comprehend, and wider than I could think. It has led me to be more willing to enter into a place of not knowing, not grasping, and not controlling. Among the gifts of the stroke was the acknowledgement of my vulnerability. In the shattering I was opened to a powerful mystery, and it has deepened by own spirituality." Alan Johnson, "Shattered Into Wholeness," in *The Lutheran Magazine* (October 2008), 30.

7. Jean Vanier in "Message," an interview with Lydia Talbot on the Chicago Sunday Evening Club's *30 Good Minutes*, program #4321, aired February 24, 2002, http://www.csec.org/csec/sermon/vanier_4321.htm, accessed July 1, 2009.

8. Robert Kennedy, quoted on *God's Politics*, blog, "Voice of the Day," http://blog.beliefnet.com/godspolitics/2006/12, accessed December 26, 2006).

9. Herschberger, *A Christian View of Hospitality*, 187.

10. Ruth Smeltzer, quoted on *God's Politics*, blog, "Voice of the Day," http://blog.beliefnet.com/godspolitics/2007/10, accessed October 9, 2007).

11. Isaiah 58:6–7.

12. Craig Rennebohm, *Souls in the Hands of a Tender God* (Boston: Beacon, 2008), 6.

13. Coffin, *Letters*, 43.

14. Etty Hillesum, quoted by Marc Ellis, *Toward a Jewish Theology of Liberation*, on *God's Politics*, blog, "Voice of the Day," http://blog.beliefnet.com /godspolitics/2007/01, accessed January 31, 2007.

15. John Petrakis, "On Film," *The Christian Century* (April 22, 2008), 41.

16. James 1:2.

17. Bayard Rustin, quoted on *God's Politics*, blog, "Voice of the Day," http://blog.beliefnet.com/godspolitics/2006/12, accessed December 20, 2006.

18. Macrina Wiederkehr, *A Tree Full of Angels: Seeing the Holy in the Ordinary* (New York: HarperSanFrancisco, 1988), 37.

19. Reinhold Niebuhr, *The Essential Niebuhr: Selected Essays and Addresses* edited by Robert McAfee Brown (New Haven, Conn.: Yale University Press, 1987), 251.

20. Coffin, *Letters*, 168.

21. Newman, *Untamed Hospitality*, 24.

22. Magalit Isabelo, quoted on *God's Politics*, blog, "Voice of the Day," http://blog.beliefnet.com/godspolitics/2008/09, accessed September 2, 2008.

23. Russell Baker, "Will the Media Be the End of Us?" *Harvard International Journal of Press Politics* 4.3 (1999), 102.

24. Clodovis Boff, quoted on *God's Politics*, blog, "Voice of the Day," http://blog/beliefnet.com/2008/09, accessed September 5, 2008.

25. John Ruskin, quoted in Coffin, *Letters*, 140.

26. Thornton Wilder, *Our Town* © 1938, in *3 Plays* (New York: HarperPerennial, 1957), 100.

27. Anaïs Nin, *The Quotations Page*, http://www.quotationspage.com/quote/27655.html.

28. John A. Sanford, *Ministry Burnout* (New York: Paulist Press, 1982), 104–05. In this image of a lake, he says, "A person must also have a source of energy, just as a lake must have a source of energy. A human being cannot always pour energy out; there must also be times when energy comes back in" (104). In this book, he has articulated many resources for spiritual growth and depth.

29. John A. Sanford, *The Kingdom Within: The Study of the Inner Meaning of Jesus' Sayings* (New York: J.P. Lippincott, 1970, 15–16.